A Year in HineSight

A Year in HineSight

Anne Hines

McArthur & Company
Toronto

This paperback edition published in Canada in 2003
by McArthur & Company

McArthur & Company
322 King St. West, Suite 402
Toronto, Ontario
M5V 1J2

First published in 2002 by McArthur & Company

National Library of Canada Cataloguing in Publication

Hines, Anne, 1958-
        A year in hinesight/Anne Hines.

ISBN 1-55278-311-1 (bound) – ISBN 1-55278-359-6 (pbk.)

1. Canadian wit and humor (English). I. Title.

PS8565.I63Y42 2002   C818'.5402   C2002-903439-6

Composition/Jacket Design & f/x: Mad Dog Design Inc.
Printed in Canada by Transcontinental Printing Inc.
Photography: Janet Bailey
Photo p. 145: Liz Early

The publisher would like to acknowledge the financial support of the
Government of Canada through the Book Publishing Industry Development
Program, the Canada Council, and the Ontario Arts Council for our publishing
activities. We also acknowledge the Government of Ontario through the
Ontario Media Development Corporation Ontario Book Initiative.

10 9 8 7 6 5 4 3 2 1

for women everywhere

May we live with faith,
love with courage
and laugh whenever we can.

Contents

This book would not have been possible without the support of:

- My "focus group" — Keltie, Kathryn, my mother, Liz, Cheryl and Avi — all of whom listened patiently through many phone calls that began "Can I read you something?"

- My much esteemed and blessedly pedantic editor, Caroline Connell.

- *Canadian Living* and *Chatelaine* magazines, for allowing me to use article titles created by their talented staff.

- Bernice Hines, for very kindly proofreading the manuscript.

- And the women who have nurtured *HineSight* in print — Bonnie Baker Cowan, Arlene Stacey, Rona Maynard, Beth Hitchcock and Kim McArthur.

I also wish to thank my children, Matt and Becky, and the rest of my family and friends who generously allow me to share their stories.

And, Liz and Judith for their unfailing encouragement.

Things I couldn't figure out how to work into the main part of the book, so I thought I'd just put them here and call it The

Introduction

I am a great believer that how you phrase something makes all the difference. As a humour writer, for instance, I know that there can be 50 ways to say something and only one of those will be funny. Sometimes I don't quite find it. When it comes to the last four years of my life — the period covered in this book — I realize that I say I will never buy my kids a dog and then end up with a dog, talk about the joys of marriage and then plunge merrily into a discussion of life after my divorce, complain about the time pressures of family life and then lament the fact that my children, Matt and Becky, are growing up and don't need me so much anymore. To some, a person who makes these shifts in thought without this simply being the result of her medication wearing off could be called "indecisive." I prefer to think of her instead as having a talent for embracing change. There is a reason I am able to do this. I don't usually have a choice.

The last four years have also made me a believer in the importance of sharing the trials and triumphs of life with friends. The greatest pleasure of writing about my life has been to hear from women who swear I am writing about theirs. It reminds me that even when we're alone in the mall or the gynecologist's stirrups, we're really all in this together.

So, thank you for joining me in this celebration of the changes and cycles of life, the seasons and the laundry. And for the chance to share some laughter together, in *HineSight*.

Note: The pieces from Canadian Living *and* Chatelaine *are arranged in seasonal rather than chronological order. So, when I refer to Michael as my husband, my ex-husband, and then my husband again, they are all one person. As if life wasn't confusing enough, eh?*

Autumn

September

There is an age-old wisdom that says nothing new can begin unless something else is ended. I apply this saying to much of my life except, of course, home renovation projects or knitting.

Fall brings the year to a magnificent close. Crisp mornings in the park with the dog. A faint icing of what might be frost or just dew that stays a little longer on the grass before the sun is warm enough to shoo it away. The green of the trees mellowing through shorter days and cool evenings into the shades of wine and sunsets.

Autumn is, without question, my favourite season, which is odd because normally I don't like endings. They seem so final. Anyone who has ever had a child or been a child knows though that September is not about endings; it's about beginnings. My own children, Matt (15) and Becky (12), turn almost unconsciously from fishing rods and swimming fins to spotless backpacks, gleaming ruled paper, and pencils sharpened to a pin. Their minds, like the pages of their new unmarked notebooks, are ready to record the facts and figures, dreams and disappointments this new school year will bring.

My neighbour Cheryl prepares her daughter Sarah for junior high and her home for Rosh Hashanah, the celebration of the Jewish New Year. Cheryl says the ritual of dipping apples into honey celebrates the harvest while promising a sweet year ahead. The Jewish calendar has three new years, in fact — a reminder, I think, that we are always beginning.

I muck about in the backyard planting tulip bulbs as my way of marking the hope that comes with new beginnings. Bulbs are tokens of my trust that spring will come again. Truthfully, though, I don't know why I bother planting them; I should just put them in a big bowl and leave them out for the squirrels. The exotic bulb mixture I buy might as well be labelled "squirrel buffet." The demise of the squirrels is something I could handle with some cheerfulness. I did a humour spot on *Canadian Living Television* in which I agreed that squirrels are "God's little creatures, too" but nonetheless fantasized about blowing them up in my garden. Needless to say, we got calls about that show. Mostly from gardeners who wanted to know if blowing up squirrels was legal.

My gardening career is also just at the beginning. I started to garden a year ago. My first time out I got a twig stuck in my eye and had to be taken to the hospital. Gardening is not really the relaxing activity it's made out to be.

On the surface, gardening looks as if it should be easy. You mess about in dirty, rumpled clothing, apparently not doing anything much at all and yet somehow, almost miraculously, producing results. I figured life as a free-lance writer had prepared me for this.

The winter before I took this on as a serious hobby I read lots of books. A couple of them were actually about gardening. The rest had gardens in them, I think. I tend, though, to be the kind to just plunge right into things without much advance preparation. I'm of the school that says that the less you know about what's involved in a new enterprise, the more likely you are to do it. It's amazing what you can sometimes accomplish before you find out it's not possible.

The first year, I have to admit, my yard looked like a home for wayward plants. Odd vines and creepers I certainly did not recognize from my seed packets put down root, flourished and rampaged over my annuals. Small buds I nurtured tenderly through the frosts of May decamped under the fence into Cheryl's garden. Hostas described as "easily transportable" were not. The rule of thumb (and certainly not a green one) seemed to be that the amount of money I paid for a green thing was in direct disproportion to the length of time it would live.

Gardening isn't the first new thing I've begun by just plunging into it. I have a long history of taking on jobs I am totally unqualified to do. Being a parent is only one of them. I have also been a community newspaper editor, managed a theatre company and waited tables. I didn't have a clue how to do any of those things.

My career as a waitress started at the beginning of my first year of university. One day, it simply came to me that it might be fun to get a part-time job in the school pub. The fact that I had never been in a bar before didn't stop me for an instant. I have no idea to this day what possessed me to get a job in the pub. I could have got a job in the school library. I had been in a library. Or the cafeteria. I had a long-standing association with food. I think I chose the school pub because it would be different.

I grew up in a strict Baptist family where we were so busy frantically trying to avoid the sins of wearing nail polish in church or going to a movie on Sunday that the sin of drinking never entered our minds. My parents certainly never touched alcohol when I was a child. When I was a teenager, they suddenly started having wine with dinner. I always wondered what made my parents start drinking. Of course, now I have teenagers of my own.

So, there I was. First day at university. First shift at the pub. First day of school also for several thousand students, all of whom, it seems to me, were dehydrated rugby players. I was the only waitress. We could fit two hundred people comfortably in that bar; I think that day there were fifteen thousand. Regardless, I approached this new challenge with perfect confidence. There's a reason for that: I was an idiot.

I would hustle up to the bartender yelling, "I need 14 Blues and 10 Pilsners." They're the same thing. "I need a Tom Jones and some kind of carpentry tool!" He handed me a Tom Collins and two screwdrivers. It came as a revelation to me that the guys at the back weren't planning repairs to their bar stools.

Things got a bit tense with my clientele. In fact, I've seen more generosity of spirit at an anti-apartheid rally. When my shift finally ended, it was time to mark the occasion with another first: a stiff drink.

I worked part-time in the pub for the whole of my four years at school. With lots of hard work and concentration I eventually worked myself up to the level of "marginally competent." My proudest achievement at university may well have been that I could remember five tables of drink orders at a time. I could even typecast guys by the kind of beer they drank. I thought of writing a manual: "Carlsberg drinkers: are kind and attentive; the type of guys you marry . . . the second time around. Blue drinkers: will be watching the ball game during your wedding reception." I also learned that in a world without women, the beer glass industry would collapse entirely (along with, I might add, the beer coaster business and probably the companies who manufacture laundry detergent).

Over four years, among the pub's 20 or so tables, I learned a lot about endings and beginnings. Girls and guys met, dated, broke up, drowned their sorrows and found their next true love. Teams rejoiced or brooded and planned what they'd do to "them" next year. Friendships formed that would last forever or a single term. Ideas and plans took root and sprouted, minds and lives blossomed as we all prepared to enter the world beyond the university walls. The pub was a study in dreams and hope — the things you really need to make a new beginning.

This fall, 20 years after I graduated, I returned to the same university as a student. I don't have to wait tables this time, which is a shame, because having raised a family I now have the experience to do it. I figure I could also qualify for a job as the campus social convener, ethics commissioner, guidance counsellor or janitor. I don't spend any time at the school pub now. It's been a revelation to find, in fact, that the institution also offers classes. The biggest difference in starting school this time, though, is that I now know enough to be daunted.

Someone wiser than I said, "If you want to improve, you must be prepared to appear foolish." At this rate, I figure I'll be perfect by Christmas. I have to admit I feel out of place as I shoulder my knapsack and make my way across the university grounds. Physically, everything about the school is the same as I remembered except that they now appear to be running a daycare. There are students in my classes who weren't yet born when I graduated the last time. I find myself doing the same things that used to astonish me about the mature students of my day: turning up for all the classes and asking questions that show that I might actually have done the reading.

What I have on my side this time is experience. I now know that new adventures do come with some guarantees. I'm pretty well guaranteed, for instance, that sometimes this is going to be tough. I'm also guaranteed that I'm going to learn something. Perhaps that's the biggest difference of starting something new at this stage of life; I've come to think that's a fair trade-off.

September leaves drift across the campus, announcing the year that is ending, and I have to smile. Once again, I'm just at the beginning.

Deck the Malls

September! With it comes that big moment we've been waiting for all summer, an event filled with anticipation, anxiety, hope and fear. I refer, of course, to the start of Christmas shopping.

I admit that Christmas shopping in September is ridiculous. I should have started in June. To find special memorable gifts for the people I love, I have to start early. I've bought many special memorable gifts over the years. I just can't remember any of them at the moment.

Shopping for my husband, Michael, is a challenge. 'Round about this time of year, I say things like, "Do you need new slippers?" He says yes and goes out and buys them.

I read that shopping early saves money. I canvassed the stores to see what was available and who had the best prices, and then went home and made a list of people to shop for, items to buy and what they would cost. This did cut down on spending; by the time I got back to the store, everything I wanted was gone.

Some people do put off Christmas shopping until it's actually Christmas. There's a name for these people — they're called men.

My older brother is an excellent example of this kind of shopper. Bruce's philosophy of life is that there are few events so important or so serious that they cannot be turned into a sports event. During long church services when we were kids, Bruce used to keep us entertained by handicapping the talents of the choir members. Our tenor, Mr. Finley, was in constant danger of being sent down to the minors. Bruce's approach to Christmas shopping is to start at one end of a mall at 4 p.m. on Christmas Eve and see how far he can get before 6 p.m. If you receive a gift in a drugstore bag, you know he didn't make it to your name before the mall closed.

My own Christmas shopping routine goes like this.

August: Buy lovely, thoughtful gifts for my two sisters and hide them away. Feel smug. Ignore list for rest of the month.

September: Cannot find list. Make new one. Kids want Rocket Billy dolls at $49.99 each. Will wait till they go on sale. Buy lovely, thoughtful gifts for my two sisters. Remember I already got them something. Wonder if gifts could be given to children's teachers instead. They are both men. Darn. Need to regroup. Abandon shopping efforts.

October: Determined to start immediately. At first store, buy Halloween candy, decorations, costumes and cards. Enough shopping. Have coffee. Go home.

November: Really serious now. March into store and buy lovely, thoughtful gifts for my two sisters. Darn. Wonder if free sample that came with makeup purchase could be given to best friend without her knowing. Break down and decide to buy Rocket Billy dolls. Stores are out of stock. Company spent so much on advertising, it could only afford to make six. Believe clerk who says, "We're getting more next week."

Early December. Have become source of entertainment to toy store clerks. "Hey, Joey! This lady wants to know if we have any Rocket Billy dolls!" Cannot mail holiday cards because have not put personal, handwritten note in each yet.

Mid-December. Hate everyone on list. Would pay almost anything for a Rocket Billy doll but not the $300 being asked for in the newspaper. Consider becoming Eastern Orthodox to gain two extra weeks of shopping.

Late December: Will buy anything for anyone. See everything as potential gift. "Hmm . . . masking tape. Maybe Michael would like masking tape." Realize I now have to wrap all this stuff. Have completely forgotten where I hid gifts bought in August. Have not mailed Christmas cards. Decide it's like wedding gift thank-yous; if you get them out within a year of the event, it's OK. Put on John Denver Christmas album, severely spike eggnog and try to forget.

Christmas Day: Everyone loves everything! Such a joy to give gifts to the people I love! Vow to address and mail cards ASAP.

Next year I will start much, much earlier!

Dogged by Turtles

It's autumn and my family has already begun their time-honoured Christmas tradition: trying to convince me to buy a dog. The whining and coaxing start just after Labour Day — they learned that from toy advertisers.

I'm an advocate of the rule that says you shouldn't give a dog as a Christmas gift. I believe the same thing about dogs as birthday gifts, Valentine gifts, Hanukkah gifts, gifts for the Chinese New Year or to honour the feast day of the mother goddess Akua'ba.

Don't get me wrong, I love dogs. I love the idea of being the focus of ceaseless, unquestioning adoration; it's why I got married. But I'm not sure I'm cut out to be a dog owner. I can't see myself bonding with something that will never be toilet-trained. And, I am not a morning person. I'm kind of a 3-to-3:15-in-the-afternoon person.

I'm all in favour of the kids learning responsibility. I've explained to Matt and Becky that if we're going to have a pet, it has to be one that fits into our lifestyle — in other words, able to survive with only random feedings and prepared to help out with the laundry.

As a family, we've had some experience with pet ownership. A few years ago, we bought turtles. Both my husband and I had Red-eared Slider turtles when we were children. They lived for about three months. Then their shells turned mushy and they died or they crawled under the radiator and were never seen again. We preferred to think they had found freedom and I suppose, in a way, they did.

The great thing about turtles is that children have the pleasure of receiving a pet. Yet they are relieved, after a short time, of the responsibility of looking after their pets, and a valuable life-lesson (Things Die) is learned. Of course, my children were already familiar with this life lesson — they'd seen my garden.

We headed off to buy the requisite plastic turtle dish with the little plastic palm tree, remembered from my husband's youth and mine. The plastic palm tree is key. It makes the turtles think they are still in their natural habitat. We figured the whole thing — with turtles — would cost about six dollars.

We returned home with a total turtle ecosystem: a 10-gallon aquarium complete with water purification pump, warming lamp, floating logs for the turtles to lounge on as they tan themselves, and, of course, "turtle ambience" — coloured stones and assorted ceramic statues. The six dollars we planned to spend didn't even cover the tax.

The children refused to clean the tank once they realized that these two little critters produced in one hour about 40 times their body weight in turtle waste. I spent more hours cleaning the turtle tank each week than I did cleaning my own house. OK, that's not saying much, but during the cleaning, the turtles hissed at me ungratefully.

The children stopped going anywhere near them. I have to confess I thought I would be able to brave mushy-shell syndrome when the time came.

Sure enough, after a couple of months, the turtles' shells began to peel. I broke it gently to the kids.

"The turtles might be ill."

"What turtles?"

Suddenly, the peeling stopped.

I telephoned the Aquatic Animal Consultant at Pet Palace who assured me that peeling was a normal part of the turtle growth cycle. Apparently, the turtles would grow to be over a foot long and live about 30 years. He told me not to worry.

The only thing that kept me going in the months following was the thought that when the children left for university in 10 years, I would make them take the turtles with them. Then a friend announced that she was directing a play in another city and needed a live turtle. The larger of our two turtles got the part. It hissed and spit at the other actors for weeks and finally escaped into a nearby pond. Our understudy turtle was shoved onstage on opening night without a rehearsal.

The local paper ran a full account.

Pet ownership taught me a lot about responsibility. I have a responsibility to keep myself sane. The day will come when my children will be mature and reliable enough to care for a dog. And when that time comes, they'll explain to their children that a pet is a big commitment for a busy household. In the meantime, I'm giving the people I love a gift they can enjoy on any occasion. A happier, calmer me.

School Daze

The longer I am a parent, the more I learn. Mostly, I learn how I should have done everything completely differently. On Becky's sixth birthday, for instance, I learned never to have a birthday party for six-year-olds. When Matt dyed his hair green at age 13, I learned that wash-out colour certainly does not.

The area in which I have probably learned the most is in my children's schooling. The more years my children spend in school, the better educated I become. Having now parented two children through elementary school, I feel ready to pass on information that every parent needs.

Field Trips

At some point in your child's school life you will probably find yourself on a field trip. The purpose of these excursions is to expose the students to sites of cultural or historical interest so that when the time comes for a family outing, they can go bowling instead. A few children will be assigned to your care for the day. Take a good look at your group; it is the last time you will see them.

You may wish to prepare some key phrases to use with the children to help them get the most out of their trip experience — things like "Get down from there," "No, it's not time for lunch" and "Does your mother let you do that at home?"

It is a basic truth of field trips that out of any group of six children, two will need to use the washroom at any one time. But at some point during the day you'll come across something that really mesmerizes the students and captures their attention. Usually it's the gift shop. Some parent volunteers won't allow their group into the gift shop, but I believe it's an important part of any field trip. That's where they sell the Aspirin.

Fundraising

Most schools now participate in fundraising activities to pay for little extras like textbooks and teachers' salaries. Our school sells cookie dough, frozen pizzas and chocolate-covered almonds. A family's school spirit can be directly measured by how much weight they gain in a year. I've often thought a better fundraising scheme would be to have people pay you money *not* to sell them cookie dough, frozen pizzas or chocolate-covered almonds.

Working on these projects has made me realize how vital it is to attend parent association meetings when fundraising plans are discussed. If you don't; they will vote you onto the volunteer team again.

The Playground

It is absolutely true that a child's school years provide an education that lasts a lifetime. If you're lucky, they'll also pick up a few things in the classroom. Most of what they learn, however, happens in the playground. When Matt started nursery school, I recall smugly telling the other parents that my son had no idea who the Teenage Mutant Ninja Turtles were. By the end of the first week he was calling the cat Michelangelo and we were wallpapering his bedroom with pictures of martial arts weapons.

In many ways, the playground was a difficult, disturbing new world for Matt. Becky has it easier. As the second child, she was used to random, unexplained acts of violence. Child development specialists remind us that a parent's role is to prepare our children for the world, not to protect them from it. My experience has been that with commitment and determination, you can learn to ignore that kind of advice altogether. Certainly I want my children to be independent. I just think I should be with them when they do it. Of course, there's a word for the joy, unfairness and confusion my children encountered in the school playground: *life*.

School has been an education for all of us. I admit I am sometimes a reluctant student. But I have come to see that the best thing I can teach my children is that there are things they will have to learn for themselves. So along with notebooks and pencil crayons, I will try to give Matt and Becky the tools that will truly help them to learn: faith in their own abilities, confidence to face new experiences and the knowledge that with all its challenges and uncertainty, it is an exciting world out there.

I think we're all in for another wonderful year of learning.

October

A *trip* *to* *the* *mall* and you can tell it's almost Halloween: I have to fight my way through the Christmas displays to get to the costumes. If you ask me, there's a problem with how retail stores approach the big holidays: it's all so commercial.

Christmas seems to arrive in the stores a little earlier every year. It may be T-shirt weather outside but retailers think if they put out the glitter and ornaments I'll suddenly be rushing to line up to buy Christmas decorations in October. I am not so easily manipulated; I always wait for an empty cash desk.

After slogging my way through the mall, I decided to take myself somewhere where I could regain my sense of what's really important in life. I went to IKEA.

I love IKEA. I've spent entire afternoons wandering through those showrooms. Mostly because that's how long it takes to get to the cash desk.

Those beautiful IKEA showrooms really do reflect my lifestyle. Not how it is, of course, but how it should be. At IKEA, things sparkle. Impossible dreams seem suddenly entirely possible. Dreams such as finally figuring out how other people match stripes and florals without their bedroom looking like a jail for flowers, or being able to completely transform my living-room décor with decorative throw pillows, or that eight-piece dinette set actually fitting into my trunk.

Also, the whole IKEA concept is just so sensible. For the tiny inconvenience of trekking through eighteen hundred miles of furniture to get to the section you want, hunting for someone to write up your order, waiting for the box, hauling it to your car, dragging it off your car, then into the house, and putting it all together yourself, you can save as much as $10 on a bedroom suite.

I have no time for cynics who complain that "IKEA" is Swedish for "out of stock." I have never had any problems like that . . . almost . . . well, one time I didn't. I have to admit, the rest of the time I've waited in line 25 minutes to speak to a salesperson only to be told that, unless I place an order, they won't tell me whether or not they have the item in stock. To me, this is a little like having to accept a marriage proposal before you can meet the guy's relatives. Who knows what you're getting into?

This time, I decided to buy a bookshelf. I do not actually need a bookshelf. I need about two hundred. Books seem to get into my workroom and multiply. However, one bookshelf was all I could afford at the moment. The salesperson used IKEA's very efficient computer stock-control system to tell me exactly what the dimensions of the bookshelf were, what colours it came in, how much it cost, how much my quality of life would improve once I owned it and that it would not be in stock for 6 weeks. Couldn't they just sell me the floor model? He shook his head. No, they need the floor model to show other customers what isn't available. The salesperson promised me, however, it would likely not take the usual 6 weeks for this bookshelf to be in stock. He was right. It took 10.

I have to admit that, while IKEA showrooms encourage me to dream, getting the box of furniture pieces home always lands me back in reality. Over many years of putting IKEA furniture together, I've begun to think that maybe the company just slaps the same assortment of boards and screws into these boxes and then labels them "bookshelf," "TV stand" or "dining-room suite." For all the use this collection of boards is, they might as well just hand me an axe, point me at a tree and tell me to make an armoire.

The only good time to start to put together a piece of IKEA furniture is after 11 p.m. By that time, you're already exhausted and drained, so you don't have far to go.

It seems to me that there is money to be made by someone starting a business called "IKEA Busters." This business would offer three services:

Service #1 (early evening): People pay you to come to their house and bring them the C24 Allen key, which the instructions indicate is included in the box and which is absolutely not included in the box, so that they can put the thing together.

Service #2 (after midnight): People pay you to bring the C24 Allen key and put the thing together for them.

And Service #3 (as dawn stretches her transforming fingers across a gently lightening sky): People pay you to come and take the damn thing away so they will never have to look at it again.

The downside of this business would be, of course, the hours. Before 1 a.m., most people still believe that Side A might actually be coaxed into standing upright holding Piece C, regardless of everything they've ever heard about gravity. The upside is that everyone you served would be in exactly the right frame of mind to be good customers: desperate. By 4 a.m. you could forget about the fee schedule and negotiate a deal. Something like, "Sorry, we don't take VISA. Gosh, that's a really nice car in your driveway."

This time, I had my bookshelf completely assembled by 6 a.m. It wasn't exactly like the one I'd seen in the showroom. That one would actually hold books. But it had one thing that showroom bookshelf did not have — I'd put it together myself. No, this wasn't much consolation.

The only upside to this project is that I got a few rare hours alone to think about my life. Mostly I thought things like "I will spend the rest of it looking for the person who did not put a C24 Allen key in this box."

I also realized that IKEA furniture is not the only thing in my life that forces me to continually reconcile the way things are supposed to be with the way things actually are.

Take the process of aging, for example. My expectation is that, regardless of the trillions of dollars spent by the makers of cosmetics, face creams and anti-aging schemes to convince me that only youth is beautiful, I will have the inner strength to choose to age confidently and naturally. I work hard to send myself the message that wrinkles give character and beauty is more than taut skin and smooth buttocks, but most days it's a losing battle. Frankly, I just don't have their kind of budget.

Motherhood is also a continual challenge of reconciling expectation with reality. IKEA furniture comes with one set of instructions. As a mother, everyone you meet is prepared to give you a different set altogether.

Sixteen years ago, when I was expecting my first child, I read all of the newest books on the wonders of motherhood and I knew exactly the way pregnancy should be. I would glow. I would suddenly become aware of my power as an earth goddess and my cosmic, intuitive connection to all other female beings. I would wish to eat organic beets.

None of that happened. Out of a list of 120 awful conditions your body may develop during pregnancy, I think I got 119. I wished only to eat beef jerky. If I glowed, it was because I was face down in the toilet most of the time. The books assured me that this was a mystical time in my life. The only mystery to me was why anyone would do this more than once. I remember longing for the baby to be born so that my life could get back to normal. Number 121 on the list should have been "you'll be incredibly naive."

Then came labour. Now, my reading material promised, I was entering a brief and euphoric moment in my life. I felt like I spent 24 hours trying to pass a bowling ball. By the time our son was born, my husband and I had decided that if I ever got pregnant again, neither of us wanted to be present at the birth. Michael speculated that there's probably some correlation between the national birth rate dropping at exactly the same time that fathers were expected to be present in the labour room.

My days as a young mother were not what I expected either. There I was, 24 hours a day with this tiny person who I loved with every fibre of my being, and I'd never felt more alone.

I was invited to a mothers' support group. I was anxious to go. At that point in my life, I couldn't get enough support from my bra, let alone the people around me. The woman who invited me said that we'd all sit around and share our birthing stories. I assumed this was to make sure we never did it again.

I realized in the first two minutes that I just wasn't like these women. These were women who hand-made their diapers out of unbleached organic cotton. Women who were planning to breast-feed until their children entered high school. My policy was that I didn't breast-feed anything with teeth. The women discussed how disappointing it would have been to have had drugs during labour. I wanted the drugs. I wanted all the drugs. The woman who gave me an epidural is still in my will. My children are now 12 and 15 and I *still* want the drugs.

There was no way I was ever going to fit into this group. I stuck a soother in my child's mouth, slapped a disposable diaper on his bottom and announced I was going home to cook red meat.

When Matt and Becky were still infants, I went back to my job managing a theatre company. I was now classified as a "working mother." I'm not sure what I had been when I was at home with the kids. Eventually, I started working from a home office, which is basically the same thing as working outside the home, except no one else ever makes the coffee.

There was no longer any question of reconciling expectation with reality. I couldn't figure out anymore what the expectations were. I knew I was supposed to be home with my kids, making zoo animals out of milk cartons and baking cookies from spelt flour I ground myself. I also knew I was supposed to be out contributing to the family income and earning the right to be asked my opinion about anything. I envied a childless colleague of mine who didn't have to deal with the kind of guilt I was struggling with. She said she felt guilty for not having kids.

From what I could make out of all of this, what my life should look like was actually quite clear. I should pursue a challenging career while staying home with my children. Similarly, I am now supposed to retain a youthful appearance while rising above the use of products and procedures that would make that vaguely possible. And, I must nurture my own spirit and sanity while attending to the needs of every other person in the world first.

When I put it all together now, I find that this is not at all a mixed message. I must simply be all things to all people at all times. If I do that, the reward will be worshipful, adored sainthood. Frankly, that's not enough.

The truth is, I think, that in the end my life is a lot like IKEA furniture. There is the expectation of how it ought to look and then there is what's actually possible. In the case of my bookshelf — if it's still standing, I think I've done a good job. In the case of my life as a whole — if I make it through the day, sometimes falling short, sometimes meeting my own needs before my children's, sometimes finding what is beautiful in living the unexpected rather than the expected, I will be doing pretty well. Of course that's not the way life is supposed to be. To my mind, it's better.

Fit for Life

NOTE: *A reader pointed out to me that putting cayenne on your flower bulbs is harmful to squirrels. Please just read and enjoy, but don't follow my lead on this one!*

I have come to the realization that on the scale of Women Who Run With the Wolves, I am Woman Who Lets Out the Cat.

The thought occurred to me last night as I flipped through the television channels, wondering if watching Yugoslavian junior table tennis meant I was just too tired to get up and go to bed. Suddenly, I came across a documentary titled *Amazing Things Other Women Did While You Were Wondering If It Was Blue Box Day*, or something like that. The program featured women who had climbed Everest, been shot into outer space or free-fallen 3,000 metres from an airplane. My first thought was, "So what? All my days feel like that." And then I thought that just maybe my life could be more exciting.

I don't usually feel that there could be more to life. Usually I feel that there could be less — less laundry, less work, and as I look out into the yard, less squirrels. The squirrels must be digging up the bulbs from my garden and planting them across the street, where all my neighbours have beautiful gardens. I tried shaking cayenne pepper on the bulbs last year but I swear the little critters just thought I was serving Tex-Mex.

There could also be fewer holidays. I don't mean less vacation time. In the midst of long periods of frantic activity, vacations are precious moments of frantic activity while wearing a bathing suit. But between getting the kids back to school in September and preparing for the holidays in December, Halloween is playing a bigger role than ever. My next-door neighbour Cheryl says, "Try fitting Rosh Hashanah and Yom Kippur into that, too!" I have two words for her — *Christmas shopping*.

Outfitting my son, Matt, for Halloween was never a problem. Black sweat-pants and a large plastic weapon and he was happy. My daughter, Becky's, requests have always been more challenging. Stores can be crammed with ready-made princess and super hero costumes and she'll want to go out dressed as a paperclip. I'm hoping there's a special heaven for craft-challenged parents who still manage to make a Halloween costume that looks like something. Mind you, the something my costumes always looked like was the pumpkin outfit my neighbour gave me four years ago, but surely it's the thought that counts.

It is possible, though, that I could use a little more excitement in my life. The most interesting thing I did this week was to sign the organ donor form when I got my new health card. It was a distinct thrill to know that someone wants my body. I told the clerk that I have some fat cells I am prepared to donate immediately, but the Ministry doesn't accept them.

I have to admit, that at this stage of life, living dangerously means drinking caffeinated coffee after 8 p.m. or putting down white carpet in the living room. Spontaneity is anything that happens with less than a week's notice for the babysitter.

A need for excitement came over me last fall as well. I finally climbed the walls. I mean, I went to a climbing gym and actually climbed the walls. Not quite Everest, but when I was six metres above the floor, hanging by my fingernails, the difference seemed insignificant. My 20-year-old instructor Skip, who works as a bicycle courier during the day, kept yelling up, "Work from your stomach muscles." I don't have stomach muscles. I traded them 11 years ago for children. At one point I was clinging to a tiny indentation, sweating profusely and listening to Skip discuss from the ground how to get a middle-aged woman off a wall. All I could think was, "Well, I'm not bored anymore."

In my world, conquering Everest means tackling the mountain of papers on my desk or laundry in the basement. These days if I want to broaden my horizons, I keep my feet on the ground and take in a lecture at the library. If I'm still desperate for excitement, I may just try the classic solution: a new haircut. It might not be jumping out of a plane, but I defy anyone to tell my nervous system the difference.

The truth is, I have all the challenge I need just keeping up with work and family life and finding time for an occasional quiet moment alone. My life may never be exciting enough to warrant a documentary, but trying to lead a sane, caring and responsive life means that, really, there's never a dull moment.

Feudal Laws

I'm taking a moment to congratulate myself on my fabulous parenting skills. With any luck, it will take my mind off the sound of the kids fighting downstairs.

Matt and Becky don't argue 24 hours a day. Sometimes they're asleep. The rest of the time they seem to be either bugging each other or plotting to bug each other. There are five star military strategists who have nothing on my kids.

I can't remember when my kids started arguing with each other.

Probably around the moment they could talk. My mother told me to be patient, things would change. They did. They got worse.

While I never expected my kids to be best friends, I admit I was unprepared for the day when three-year-old Matt wanted to put newborn Becky into the recycling box so that she could be taken away and made into something useful.

Parenting books have helpful tips such as "You can eliminate sibling discord by encouraging your children to share similar goals." Mine do — each wants to be an only child. Experts also say that children fight to get attention. This is a myth, just like "You can breathe through the pain." Teasing is to kids what eating is to me. Sure, sometimes there's a purpose, but most of the time it's purely recreational.

I grew up in a very close family. With five children in one house, close was our only option. Wherever we were going, whatever we were doing, it was a group outing. It meant I was well prepared for motherhood; I'd never been alone in the bathroom in my life.

Bruce, Keltie and I were all born two years apart. Then, as my mother puts is, "After Anne came, we needed a rest." David was born five years later, and five years after that we adopted Kathryn. Kathryn is fond of saying, "They had to take you. They picked me out special." We knew she was right.

Having brothers and sisters teaches many key life skills — such as how to stay alive. Bruce liked to stand in front of my bedroom door, hunched over like a linebacker, and growl, "Try to get past me." To this day I enter rooms shoulder first. I once convinced David that if he climbed a tree behind our suburban home, he could see Dad's office in the city. I tied David securely to the branch so he wouldn't fall. Then I left. Hours later, my mother found him limp and exhausted from calling for help. He turned me in. I couldn't believe it.

We drove my parents nuts. I recall my father stopping the car on a long road trip to yell, "The next time I take you kids anywhere, I'm leaving you at home!"

We weren't alone. It wasn't uncommon in our neighbourhood to hear a parent shouting, "What did I tell you about killing your brother? Do it outside!"

The truth about squabbling is that I did it when I was young, but I don't want my kids to do it. Much like dating.

A friend of mine promised her twins a $200 videogame system if they stopped arguing for a month. She had 30 days of peace and quiet. Now they argue over the videogames.

Another woman I know took her seven-year-old and nine-year-old to a child psychiatrist.

Woman: They bicker, they fight, they make me crazy.
Learned doctor: They're kids.

It cost her $80.

The real problem with the kids' squabbling is that someone always ends up getting angry and frustrated. Me. Arguing doesn't seem to bother them at all. One minute they're at each other's throats, the next minute they're each other's closest friend.

My kids have taught me a lot. Love is not always patient, kind or peaceful. Sometimes it's crabby, tired and just plain unfair. The people with whom I can argue, squabble and be at my worst, yet still come through loving, are the people I value most.

Where parenting is concerned, I think I will focus my energy on gaining patience, not peace. My children will battle and make up and battle again. They're teaching each other to be human.

November

A few magically mild days in the middle of a month that really only owes us storms and gathering cold. These warm days, which we take as a birthright in August, are a gift in November. A few stray leaves still cling to branches; tree trunks now black against a slate blue sky. The leaves are swatches of yellow sunshine on black velvet boughs.

I head out in the morning, bare-headed and with my coat undone to walk the dog in our local park. Technically, Sparky is not my dog, he's Becky's dog. Becky loves the dog. She doesn't love walking him, feeding him or bathing him, but she loves him. "If you don't look after him, we're going to give the dog back" is probably the most idle threat I've ever uttered. Right up there with "If you're not good, there'll be no Christmas this year!"

I did not want to own a dog. I fell prey to the guilt that is motherhood. In this case, we got Becky the dog when Michael and I announced that we were divorcing. I guess I should feel lucky. She would have got a pony if she'd asked for it.

I am not really a "pet person." I do not understand why, now that we've evolved to the point where we no longer live among the animals, we want to bring them into our houses. Still, I've always had this idea that "kids need pets." Mind you, I had an idea that kids need siblings and I'm not sure anyone will ever convince Matt that having Becky around is making his life better.

Over the years, we have owned a guinea pig that had an overbite and needed monthly dental treatments, mice that went walkabout (once having to be cut out of the couch upholstery and once fished out of the VCR), a chinchilla that regularly attempted daring escapes by eating through screen windows and two cats who brought moles and bats into the house and lived to be about a thousand. How much trouble could a dog be?

Actually, we didn't exactly get a dog. We got a Maltese terrier. A Maltese terrier is what you get when you don't really want a dog. Sparky weighs less than my shoe. This is God paying me back for all the times I referred to people's toy poodles and cockapoos as "rat on a rope." I now get comments on the street such as, "Does that thing run on batteries?" and "Look, honey, a squirrel on a leash." I swear I'm going to get a T-shirt that says "Wanted a border collie but had to get something hypo-allergenic."

The word *terrier* stems, I believe, from "terrible" or "terror." We now own four pounds of furry attitude. He chases trucks. He threatens to take on dogs 18 times his size. His greatest ambition is to have intimate relations with the standard poodle next door. The fact that he'd need a crane to achieve his goal doesn't dampen his enthusiasm for a moment.

Maltese terriers are called the "royalty of dogs." I can only think that's because you pay a fortune for their grooming and they behave badly in public. These are not practical dogs. Maltese terriers are white. Owning a white dog is about as practical as owning a white carpet.

We got Sparky in November two years ago. I admit it's hard to bond with a dog that you're trying to house-train in a blizzard. After four months, he was perfectly house-trained; it was the only place he'd go. He was appalled by the idea of going outside to relieve himself in snow, cold, rain. I can't say I blamed him. The upside of the house-training period being over is that I can stop worrying about my good rugs and furniture. I no longer have any.

In the first few months I used to say to people about the dog, "We have a love/hate relationship. I'm just waiting for the love part to kick in." Sparky and I did finally manage to hammer out an agreement about how he was going to behave. The basis of this agreement is — he does whatever he wants. After raising two children, I just don't have the will or the energy to enforce rules and set limits one more time. So, the dog sleeps in my bed, demands constant attention and yaps when he's not happy. Mind you, I laid down the law with the kids and they behaved the same way.

Sparky follows me everywhere I go. Our vet explained to me that this is "pack behaviour." Sparky thinks I am his "Alpha" — the leader of his pack. I preferred not to think what it meant about my leadership that I couldn't get the "lead-ee" to do his business outside. The vet also assured me that dog training is easy because they are anxious to please. Sure — themselves. In those early days, Sparky would look me in the eye and pee on the floor.

I used to talk to myself. Now I talk to the dog. For some reason, people find this less odd. I also spend more time talking to the neighbours. Mostly I say things like "Yes, that really is full grown" and "Yes, he does make that noise all the time."

On these warm November days, Sparky curls up in a sunny spot on the grass as I rake the last of the leaves in my late fall garden. I go out and walk because he needs to go out and walk. I move at a dog's pace just as I used to move at my children's — once again every foot of sidewalk and front lawn offers adventure and wonder.

The concept of taking the dog to a park is totally outside my experience. I grew up in a rural town where there was no such thing as walking the dog. You opened the back door and the dog went out. Later on, the dog came back. Each morning now, Sparky and I go to the same park. To him, it's a fresh miracle every time. Like taking a kid to a new theme park every day.

I am now one of the "dog people." Having got to the point where I'm not just "Becky's mom" or "Matt's mom," I am now "Sparky's mom." I spend more time each day talking to other dog people than I do to my own family, and I have no idea what most of their names are.

There are dogs that get along, dogs that get jealous, dogs that should never be let off a leash; the world of human behaviour is seen more clearly in the world of furry creatures. Some things our dogs do better than we do; spats are over in seconds and never existed by the next day; alliances last forever.

The dog people stand about in a knot while the dogs sniff each other and run in circles. We sniff each other metaphorically. Besides giving me a few more grey hairs, Sparky has given me community. The dog park is full of stories and gossip, affinity and life.

A few of the dog people I know well by now. Ina, elegant, well read and widely travelled, mothers her Shih Tzu Marmalade, and tells me stories of Hungarian countesses who proclaim that "a party is never a success unless there is a chance of a marriage, a break-up or an illicit liaison." Ina's memories of gathering flowers in Morocco, falling in love in Argentina and having her fortune told by gypsies in Poland warm my imagination on cold November days. Marmalade and Sparky chase each other in circles and stalk empty plastic bottles.

Doris, who convinces me daily that life begins at 70, squeezes walks with her poodle Buster into her schedule of volunteering, work and socializing. Buster's main interest in life is eating things he finds under picnic tables. We feed our dogs carefully balanced, highly nutritious dog food and pure water and all they really want is to drink out of puddles and scarf decaying tuna sandwiches.

Jerry, the dentist, whose life's work is writing a book about faith and personal growth, talks to me of cuspids and karma. Jerry contends that we are given the dogs we need to learn life lessons. I wonder what I have learned from having Sparky. Well, that I don't want to own a dog for one thing. The other thing, strangely, seems to be about love.

As Sparky grows out of puppyhood he is learning to behave. Still, on days that he doesn't feel like leaving the park, he does his Bad Puppy Dance, darting up and away, barking defiance of my authority. He drags me out of bed on the weekend, long before I am ready. He brings me his toy to throw when I want to read the newspaper. He is annoying and dependent, demanding and yappy and will never be a border collie. And, the fact is of course, that I'm nuts about him.

I tell cute Sparky stories. I am convinced he is brilliant, even though the concept of "growling at Rottweilers/bad" continues to elude him. I toss Premium Organic Dog Dream Treats into the shopping cart beside the definitely non-organic hot dogs I'm having for lunch. If I'm in the elevator and it's more than two floors between stops, I make people look at pictures.

I am reminded, somehow, of my early years as a mother. Nothing prepared me for the exhaustion, the frustration, the relentless demands of these dependent little human beings. But, nothing prepared me, either, for how much I would love my children.

Love for this tiny, white, demanding dog comes to me like a warm day in November — unexpected and unexplained. It is a gift.

Sparky and I shiver in the park as the wind blows suddenly

cooler; the sun passing into a grey cloud may finally bring November snow. I tuck him inside my jacket and we walk past the amused grins of the big-dog owners. He snuggles in close as we head for home.

Abreast of Improvements

I seem to be having one of those days. My car tire blew, the dog has worms and I think my breasts are deflating. It's always something, right?

The car and the dog I can take care of. The breasts are more of a challenge. I admit I did pause for a moment when I was pumping up the tire — just for a moment.

More than a few years ago I had my second child. It's natural that having children means my youthful figure was gone for good, along, of course, with my memory and sanity. I did manage to get back to my pre-childbirth weight. It's just all in different places.

I've come to the conclusion that if I want my body back into shape, it's time to resort to drastic measures. Not exercise — that's too drastic. What I mean is that it's time to come to terms with the aging process, and to make that easier, I'm planning to have my breasts done.

This isn't the first time I've thought about cosmetic surgery. Back in my thirties I said that when I hit 50 I was going to get everything nipped, tucked, sucked and lifted. Of course, once I hit 40 I realized that was ridiculous — I need it now.

There are some things you're not supposed to talk about. Colouring your hair is OK. Lots of people colour their hair — except me, of course. It's normal for people's hair to get greyer with age: mine gets blonder.

But cosmetic surgery falls into the category of things people do but no one talks about, like reusing tea bags or seeing a psychiatrist. It's OK to call in a specialist to change a dimmer switch, but there's something wrong with hiring a professional to sort out your life. The first time I went for therapy, I knew instinctively that I had to find a less embarrassing excuse for why I was visiting a doctor. I said I had head lice.

My friend Kathy consulted a psychiatrist for her dog. Angus has eaten everything, including the front seat of their pickup truck. (They now have a small couch in the truck cab. We can't decide if it should be featured in *Popular Mechanics* or *Canadian House and Home*.) The doggie shrink prescribed sedatives, which worked really well until Kathy realized they were for the dog.

It's possible that my desire for perfect breasts is making mountains out of molehills. But our images of beauty are movie actresses who seem to age backward. Who cares about looking as good as Goldie Hawn did when she was 20? I want to look as good as she does now!

Last week I went to see a cosmetic surgeon. The doctor ushered me into his office and immediately tried to put me at ease.

"Don't worry, Mrs. Hines, I'm sure we can do something about that nose."

We discussed the importance of having realistic expectations.

"I want breasts," I said, "fabulous breasts. Breasts that will make *Baywatch* babes look like prepubescent boys. Breasts that will make Jamie Lee Curtis weep."

He said we could do that.

I left a half-hour later with the understanding that you can indeed have it all, and it starts at about $1,800 a side.

Thankfully, one thing does get firmer as I get older — my resolve to think for myself. I've begun to believe that my body doesn't need enhancement. Maybe someone could implant some imagination in the fashion industry, whose vision of beauty is limited to firmness and youth.

Consulting a plastic surgeon was like visiting the Wizard of Oz. While I was asking for new breasts, I suddenly realized that I should make use of what I already have — a brain and a heart. My brain tells me that there is no one sexier than a person who is at home in her own skin. My heart tells me that there is room in the world for many pictures of what is beautiful. My honey tells me I'm perfect exactly the way I am. There's no improving on that.

Muddling Through

This morning, I was sitting over a third cup of coffee, staring out at the last few falling leaves of the year, wondering why I never seem to have enough time in the day to get things done. Suddenly, I received that one phone call every parent dreads: the president of our school volunteer committee.

Madam President: Anne, it's Marjorie Cohen.

Me: Mrs. Hines is not here! She has gone on a very long trip! On the space shuttle! (OK, I didn't say that. Instead, I thought really fast and said, "Oh, um . . .")

MP: We had a meeting last night to discuss the chair of the annual fun fair and your name was mentioned.

Me (hopefully): As the *last* person you could imagine asking to do it?

MP (chuckles appreciatively): Now, we know you're busy . . .

Me (looking at half-empty coffee cup and partially eaten doughnut): Actually, I was just in the middle of something.

MP: But we just knew you would do this for your school.

Me: I would not even do this for my God!

MP: It's such a small commitment. I'll send over the boxes of instructions.

Me: But, I . . .

MP: So lovely of you to volunteer.

I do not want to chair the fun fair. It will not be fun. In previous years, in fact, we dubbed it the not-really-as-much-fun-as-you'd-think fair. I've seen parents who work in the justice system unable to keep order at the bouncy house. I've spent entire afternoons on snow-cone duty, managing a syrup dispenser that was designed to squirt at my hair, my shoes, the shoes of my fellow volunteers, pretty well everywhere — except at the snow cones.

There is a reason, of course, why I've been asked to chair the fun fair. It has to do with that old adage "If you want something done, ask a busy person" — they're so stressed out already, they're likely to agree to anything.

Also, I have somehow, inexplicably, got a reputation for being organized. I have no idea how this happened. I let people see my kitchen. I've made it known around the schoolyard that the way I keep my closets tidy is to leave our clothes in handy plastic baskets in the laundry room. And I regularly show up for events that are not scheduled and miss ones that are.

In spite of this, people seem to think I have control over my life. I don't. Fifteen years ago, I exchanged control over my life for children. I've had many discussions with friends as we pick the kids up at school — rush one to soccer practice and the other to dance class, between which we have to drop off their library books and pick up something for dinner — about how, once you have kids, you can't get anything done.

Perhaps my reputation for being organized comes from the fact that I spend my life juggling the demands of two children, a household, a job and two pets and I'm still standing at the end of the day. There is a reason for this: I'm usually too tired to go to bed.

I have tried to get more organized. But, as Phyllis Diller — whose parenting style (and, alas, hairstyle) I often seem to emulate — once said, "Cleaning your house while your children are still growing is like shovelling your walk before it stops snowing." My kids own 700 times their body weight in stuff. I've given up trying to convince them that the goal of a street garage sale is to get rid of more junk than they buy from friends. Last year, my daughter Becky came home pulling a wagon piled high with ancient, decomposing stuffed animals. She was incredulous: "They sold me all this for a dollar!" I'm still not speaking to those neighbours.

A survival technique I cling to is keeping lists. Once, when I was buried under paperwork, I did exactly what the experts suggest. I sat down and made a list of tasks in priority sequence, detailed the resources I would need, estimated the time required to do each job and made a chart for recording the tasks as I completed them. Suddenly, I had no trouble at all organizing my time — I was out of it.

Making lists is a way of trying to pretend I have some control over my life. A little self-delusion can be comforting. The last item on my to-do list is always "Have something totally unexpected and catastrophic happen so that nothing else gets done." At least it gives me something to check off at the end of the day.

What I have realized, finally, is that there is only one thing standing between me and a calm, perfectly ordered existence: life.

I recall the exact moment this thought occurred to me. I was in my car, barrelling down a highway, late for a meeting about . . . I don't remember what it was about, but it was something of vital importance to the universe. With one hand I was wolfing down a late breakfast of cold KFC chicken and with the other hand I was wrapping a birthday gift Becky needed to take to a party after school. I think I was steering with my knee.

The car radio was tuned to CBC so that I could use this "downtime" to catch up on current events. Suddenly, I heard the radio announcer say — and I remember this clearly because these words changed my life — she said, "If you don't put lime remover in your humidifier, it might spread germs."

I was stunned. I don't actually own a humidifier and I was still stunned. Just moments ago, I'd been feeling proud of myself for keeping chicken grease off the Tomb Raider wrapping paper (well . . . almost) and now here was something else I had to do.

At that point in my life, my to-do list was already pretty full with Important Life Goals, such as:

1. Exercise 1,500 times a day to obtain supermodel-like body.

2. Work to ensure that my children share my values, beliefs and worldviews. Also, they should be able to think for themselves.

3. Learn to make napkin rings out of glitter glue and pine cones so as to amaze the world.

Frankly, I hadn't got too far on any of them.

But now, suddenly, the heavens had opened. Light dawned. I had "hit the wall." Not literally, although that was bound to happen if I kept driving with my knee.

In a way, that moment was a lot like my introduction to sex. Alarming at first, but pretty soon you start to see the possibilities. I suddenly realized that no matter how organized your life is, you can't do everything. And that trying to will just leave you anxious and exhausted (that can also be applied to sex).

My outlook on life has changed considerably since that moment. The only goal on my list now is to "muddle through." And, if I'm going to achieve even that, I'm just going to have to give up doing something. I've chosen to give up worrying about the things I don't get done. Slowly, I'm learning to tell myself what a miraculous being I am for the few things I do accomplish in a day, rather than worrying about the ones I may get to.

I've also learned a few tricks for happily living a less-than-perfect life, such as:

- If you buy cupcakes and then put your own sprinkles on them you can take them to school for your child's birthday and pass them off as homemade. I know a woman who openly admits to buying her cupcakes. I haven't reached that level of enlightenment yet, but it gives me hope.

- It is possible to clean the toilet every second week instead of every week and no one will die.

- If you're wearing both shoes, you're well enough dressed.

- If your desk is so cluttered you can barely see it, it means there's still a space left on it to put stuff.

- The best way to avoid the morning rush is to sleep until noon.

Deciding to live a less-than-perfectly-organized life means I may forever be misplacing, forgetting, regrouping. The only thing I may be able to find is happiness. And for me, that's perfect.

To help determine if you have what it takes to lead a happily disorganized life, I've prepared a handy-dandy question-naire. Hey, it beats doing the laundry.

Quiz: How Happily Less-Than-Perfect Are You?

To complete this questionnaire, you will need a pen and paper.

Immediately score five points if: You can find a pen, but it's out of ink.

Score ten points if: You find a pen, it's out of ink, but you kept it anyway in case it miraculously revives at some point.

Score zero points if: You know exactly where the pen and paper are and had them ready before you started this quiz.

1. The ultimate quest in life is:
   a) to find happiness;
   b) to find your car keys.

2. If you found yourself needing more closet space, you would:
   a) cull through your wardrobe, discarding any clothing pieces not worn in the past year, cleaning and ironing them before immediately dropping them off to a local charity;
   b) convince a family member to move out.

3. What does the phrase "muddling through" mean to you?:
   a) getting through the day by a series of unorganized and ineffective methods;

b) a talent for being able to complete tasks without having to get up from your book too often.

4. Your passport is:
   a) up to date and in a safe, specially designated place;
   b) blue . . . I think.

5. The philosophy of life you most closely subscribe to is:
   a) a place for everything and everything in it's place;
   b) if it's not broken, I've probably misplaced it.

6. In order to efficiently clean under a bed, you:
   a) move the bed;
   b) think "Who looks there, anyway?"

7. Multitasking is:
   a) a cutting edge concept in 21st century business practice, which women perfected some time around the Ice Age;
   b) what you do when both kids have the stomach flu.

8. Complete the phrase "Cleanliness is next to . . .":
   a) godliness;
   b) impossible.

9. The idea of "simplifying your life" makes you think:
   a) of reclaiming tranquillity and traditional values;
   b) oh, great, something else I have to find time to do!

10. School forms and newsletters are:
    a) an effective way to disseminate information to parents;
    b) probably what's wadded up at the bottom of my child's backpack.

Scoring

Score one point for every a) answer and five points for every b) answer. Score five bonus points if you had to count your score more than once because you got distracted doing something else.

10 to 15 points: You are probably highly efficient, beautifully organized and can never come to my house.

16 to 40 points: You have the potential to be happily disorganized, but are still dangerously efficient enough to be asked to chair a subcommittee.

41 to 65 points: Congratulations! You are a happily disorganized person. You will live to a ripe, joyous old age and probably never be able to find your scissors.

Winter

December

The first snows of December fall softly outside my workroom window and suddenly there is one thing only on my mind: "What's a synonym for 'blooming'?"

As a magazine writer, I often find myself working on articles many months before they'll be published. Winter winds are howling outside my workroom window and I'm trying to write about lilacs perfuming the park in May; or the first faint whispers of spring are stirring in my garden and I'm toiling away describing leaves falling in October and the year drawing to a close. For some people, having to live out of season like this would be disconcerting, but I think it's an excellent excuse for starting my summer vacation in March.

The easiest articles to write out of season, particularly the humorous ones, are about Christmas. The deadline for a Christmas piece is usually sometime in August and, at that point in the year, Christmas still seems like a fun idea. I wiggle my toes in the sand at the cottage and assure myself happily that this year I really will hand-make my wrapping paper, and bake, and not be in a single mall at 11 p.m. the week before the 25th. I'm not sure if it's being five months away from the holiday that makes it all seem possible, or if the summer heat just goes to my head.

Occasionally, though, trying to think about Christmas when the sun is peeling the paint off my deck can be challenging. Years ago, one of the magazines I worked for did a feature on my throwing a Christmas holiday party. The accompanying photos had to be shot in summer. It was really very exciting. For an entire morning the magazine design staff decorated my living and dining rooms with tinsel and holly. They carted in boxes of wreaths, miles of garland, even a fake tree. A neighbour, watching all this from the sidewalk, shook his head, saying, "And to think I get after my wife for starting to decorate in November!"

As the afternoon blazed into one of the hottest in memory, friends gathered in my tiny, un-air-conditioned living room to be photographed standing around cheerily sipping steaming cider and wearing winter sweaters and wool pants. We ate tons of the magazine's wonderful party fare and we all sweated off 10 pounds. What I loved about this event was that it was only the end of August and I'd done my holiday entertaining for the year.

This wasn't by any means the oddest Christmas party I've hosted. One year, when Michael and I were expecting a hundred people for a holiday open house, he arrived home an hour before and started baseboarding the living room. At a Christmas dinner party, the guests arrived only moments before the fire trucks. One friend peered into my smoke-filled kitchen and asked, "Are we eating out?" We didn't. Now, when someone asks about my favourite Christmas recipes, I say, "I like the non-flammable ones."

I love Christmas. I don't always love planning it, preparing it or paying for it, but I love Christmas. For a few short weeks of the year the things of daily life are put aside, the possibility of Peace on Earth seems . . . well, possible, and the whole world seems to shiver with anticipation.

The reality, though, is that my Christmas season is far from peaceful. Almost every day I find myself thinking, "If Christmas is about home and togetherness, why am I always alone in a mall?" I suppose there's no reason I couldn't write my Christmas cards in July or wrap my gifts in September. In fact, there's really only one thing keeping me from doing that: having to do everything else. In a normal week, I manage to keep most of my life under control, but then suddenly it all falls apart when something totally unexpected happens — like a holiday.

It doesn't help that the magazines I read these days seem to be full of articles telling me I should stop rushing through my life and just enjoy what I'm doing right now.

That would be easier if I wasn't usually in the dentist's office when I read them. I think, in fact, that I really do appreciate each moment of the day. I need every one of them to figure out where I have to go next, who needs to be picked up there and whether I have time to get groceries on the way.

As Christmas rolls around, though, my life seems to go by all too quickly. Suddenly, I want to stop time in its tracks. I long for a real old-fashioned, peaceful Christmas — just like the ones I see on the cards that other people, incredibly, seem to find time to send me. The Victorian families pictured skating or gathering around the tree in those lovely traditional scenes didn't have access to a lot of store-bought foods or packaged gifts, but they did have the one thing that makes for a truly tranquil holiday: many, many servants.

I don't exactly know why I think of peace as an essential aspect of Christmas. Growing up in a family of five children, Peace on Earth was not a term we were familiar with. Christmas in my family was my sister and I playing our new 45 of Neil Diamond singing "Sweet Caroline" over and over until my mother became suicidal. Or my brother Bruce luring five-year-old David out to the driveway, strapping one of Bruce's brand new goalie pads on him and practising slapshots until my parents finally caught him. Christmas was a house full of friends, relatives and neighbours taking 15 minutes to eat the turkey dinner my mother had been lovingly preparing since 5 a.m. Christmas in our house was noise and much laughter and some tears — anticipated for weeks and over too soon.

Christmas as a grownup hasn't been any more peaceful. Each December, I choose between the chaos of having many family members in my house or the chaos of packing up and going to be with many family members in someone else's house. Every year my sisters and I sit down and say, "There has to be a better way," and every year we decide that there really isn't. My mother never complains, even though she could hang out a sign that says, "Have turkey, will travel." She's hauled fully cooked 30-pound birds to every part of the city over the years.

This past year, for the first time ever, I did get some peace on Christmas Day. My ex-husband, Michael, took the kids to his place for the afternoon and, incredibly, I had a few hours to sit alone by the fire with a cup of tea and my wonderful new books. I hated every minute of it. Which was strange because normally I'd have said that time on my own would be the best gift going. I remember times when a trip to Shoppers Drug Mart to buy hemorrhoid cream was a big outing if someone else watched the kids. One Christmas a friend gave me a gift certificate for a massage. I remember thinking, "Heck, I would have been happy with a certificate to just have a nap at that place." What I realized in that afternoon alone, though, is that it's not the noise and confusion of Christmas that makes the time rush by, it's that I so rarely stop to think about how really lucky I am to have that noise and confusion.

In a way, spending Christmas afternoon on my own made me realize how many moments go by unnoticed because we're just too busy or unaware to realize how special they are. Where, for instance, is the ritual to mark the first time after having children that you get to go to the bathroom alone? Or the first day of real summer sunshine when you'd rather risk a few new wrinkles than start hiding under a hat?

In order not to let any more special moments slip by, I've prepared a short list of notable occasions to celebrate.

The Annual "Winter's Finally Over and I Made it Through Again" Fete
Observed only in places north of the 39th parallel, the timing depending on how far north you are. In my city, for instance, this event is held a few days before the onset of fall.

"Finally Finished With Diapers" Day
This significant occasion is marked by burning $40 cash outside your local supermarket to celebrate your release from financial burden. Following this event is an accompanying celebration, normally lasting one to two years, called the *"Now We Have To Find A Washroom Every 20 Minutes"* Festival.

The "I Went to My High School Reunion and the Cutest Girl is Now Dumpy and Married to a Complete Idiot" Frolic
While acknowledging that this is an event that is often and joyously observed I, for one, cannot condone a public celebration of someone else's misfortune. You should do it behind closed doors — where, fortunately, you still have access to a telephone. The occasion is commonly marked by exchanging phone calls with former classmates, eating a box of Twinkies — because, hey, if Stacey Schneider looks like that now, why shouldn't you? — and realizing that your partner is really not so bad after all.

The Feast of "I Finally Understand What My Mother Went Through"
Can be observed at any point during parenthood, though it is a particularly popular event during the years that you have teenagers in the house. Marked by partaking of traditional family holiday fare, humble pie.

The "I Found a Bathing Suit That Looks Fabulous On Me"
Victory Dance
A festival celebrated so rarely that many claim it to be
merely the stuff of legend. Observed by feeling sorry for
those poor, dowdy *Sports Illustrated* models, tossing out
your entire beach coverup wardrobe and calling the store
to see if they have the exact same thing in 40 other colours.

Life is full of events and experiences large and small that
are special enough to notice. In a few days the rush of
Christmas shopping and wrapping, chaos and confusion
will begin for another year. But that's not quite yet.

This morning, the first snow of December is falling, blan-
keting our dirty city streets with splendour, laying to rest
the last few autumn blooms in my garden. I can stop and
watch it fall. I can raise my cup of coffee to the few, precious moments when life does not simply rush by us,
unmarked and unrecalled. And I can toast the first snow
of the Christmas season, coming to remind me that in
every life there is something to celebrate.

Peace on Earth

When we were children, our mother would take the five
of us into town on Remembrance Day to see the Christmas
window displays. Mom did her best to impress upon us
the meaning of Remembrance Day, but when we paused
at 11 o'clock for a moment of silence, a tiny part of me still
thought it was to remember that Santa was coming soon.
I don't think I was an insensitive child. It was just hard to

equate an hour's drive in the family car with a commemoration of peace.

Christmas is a big event in a child's life, but there comes a time when you realize that you're an adult — possibly the moment you hear a radio playing "Make It Christmas All Year Long" and it no longer seems like a great idea.

Truth is, Christmas overwhelms me. It's not surprising — grocery shopping overwhelms me. I can't get used to the fact that the moment I have the largest number of life choices is when I'm standing in the ketchup aisle.

Of course, Christmas is for children. I'm childish enough to think it should be for me, too. I search for ways to feel the same excitement about the holidays that I did when I was young.

One place I still get that Christmassy feeling is at our church pageant. I love the story of the first Christmas. This year, my daughter, Becky, is hoping to be a page for one of the wise men. Getting to be a page usually means putting in many years in the angel chorus, arms falling off as you endlessly hold an invisible trumpet, tinsel halo scratching a permanent impression into your forehead. Every girl wants to play Mary. Every boy wants to be a guard in Herod's court. Guards get real swords — way cooler than the staffs that they used as swords when they were shepherds.

Last year, I was asked to be on the makeup crew because "We think you're wonderful with makeup." It was very flattering until I found out that I was in charge of making people look older.

In every pageant there is one shepherd wearing socks, another playing with a Game Boy. Last year, a backdrop fell on the angels during "Silent Night." It all reminds me that imperfections can be charming— a thought I cling to as the holidays get closer.

I look forward to the pageant, because round about the middle of December, the rest of my holiday activities start to leave me somewhat stressed. I hear that wonderful old hymn "Good King Wenceslas looked out . . ." and all I can think is "Sure, while the good Queen was wrapping gifts and ordering Christmas dinner." I long for the one thing that made the Christmases of my youth so perfect: my mother did everything. I'd like to think my father helped, but men are not always good at special occasions. Every year as I watch the three wise men lay gold, frankincense and myrrh at the feet of the newborn Jesus, I hope the three wise women will arrive shortly with diapers and a car seat.

I wonder what it is about hearing this story each year that makes my Christmas. The rest of our celebration isn't all traditionally Christian. Having latkes with Cheryl and Sarah next door is as much a part of our holiday as lighting the Advent candles.

I do believe that we can still find meaning in our traditional stories. (I tell my children that the story of Noah is about how having too many pets leads to disaster. They're not buying it.) I also think that something that has lasted so long must be wise; something I'm hoping my kids will remember that as I grow older.

Possibly I empathize with the heroine. Mary makes a long, difficult trip to her husband's relatives' place. She puts up with uncomfortable sleeping arrangements and other people's animals. Unexpected visitors drop in (none of them bring food), and she doesn't get anything she can really use. In the middle of all of this, Mary is always depicted as smiling. Why? Because it's a story, of course.

Recalling the story of the first Christmas is for me what that moment of silence on Remembrance Day should have been so many years ago — an opportunity to pause and reflect on a world filled with trial, perseverance, hope and the possibility of finding peace in the midst of chaos. No wonder it makes my Christmas.

It's the story of my life.

Jangle Bells

There's an ancient East Indian saying that has remained unaltered for many centuries: "Things change." Whoever said that knew nothing about Christmas.

The festive season is here again and I'm determined to have a holiday as wonderful as those I remember from my childhood. First, I must confess that not all my childhood Christmas memories are idyllic. I was the only one of my four brothers and sisters to ever get a lump of coal in her stocking. I couldn't believe it — I'd naturally assumed that, besides the list for "naughty and nice," Santa also had one for "framed."

My fondest memory is of sitting on the couch with my brothers and sisters each Christmas Eve, listening to my father read the Christmas story from the Bible. There was something in the closeness of that moment, the breathless anticipation of the next morning that always felt like Christmas to me. Of course, the Christmases of my youth had that one element that makes every family event seem perfect — they're way in the past.

This year, I've come to the realization that there's really only one thing I need to make this holiday as perfect as the ones I remember: I need things not to change so much. Nowadays, my siblings and I consider ourselves close if we're all in the same time zone. And the last time I felt breathless anticipation on Christmas Eve was when I realized that Tab A of Barbie's Camper Van might actually fit into Slot B if I whacked it with a Nutcracker doll.

Sure, there are some areas of life in which I'm happy to entertain the idea of change (say, other people's driving habits). But at Christmas, I want everything the way it's always been.

One way I'll maintain a connection with the past is through my lifelong flair for disorganization. When the radio starts playing "It's Beginning to Look a Lot Like Christmas," my first thought is always, "It will, it will, just as soon as I have a second to take down the Easter decorations."

One thing that never seems to change is the stress of Christmas shopping. Going to a mall in December is a surefire way to bring back memories of childhood — lots of pushing and bickering. Most of the year, I don't love the mall. I am shopping-challenged. I still wander into stores in mid-August thinking it might be nice to buy a sun hat. Or I slog through the snow in March to find that the toughest footgear on offer is strappy summer sandals. No wonder we find it so hard to live in the moment — we can't buy anything we need for it.

But the mall in December is special. It's full of people who share my values and beliefs: mail order is for parking wimps and it's not only the thought that counts, it's whether or not they'll be able to tell you got it as a "gift with purchase." I have friends who rave about the ease of doing all their shopping online. Frankly, technology will impress me the day all five of my major appliances are working at the same time. Besides, online shopping is impersonal and takes away the most important part of choosing gifts for the ones you love — trying on clothes for yourself while you're doing it.

For me, braving the shopping crowds is a Christmas tradition. Traditions are wonderful things: they allow us to continue doing something long after the reason for doing it is forgotten. In our family, for instance, we have the time-honoured, carved-in-stone tradition of my mother's homemade cranberry jelly mould. Christmas would not be Christmas without a cranberry jelly mould, blazing bright as Rudolph's nose on the festive table. To my knowledge, no one has ever eaten any of that jelly mould. None of us like cranberries. My mother may very well have shellacked a mould years ago that she continues to put out season after season. But that jelly mould has one quality that makes it meaningful: it's always there.

Tradition reassures us that things don't change. They do, of course, but I've always said that a little self-delusion can be very comforting. Years ago, when my siblings and I had moved out of the family home for the fourth or fifth time, my mother mentioned in passing that she might put her Christmas tree in the family room instead of the living room, for a change. Panicked phone calls criss-crossed the country — Mom was thinking of moving the tree!

Granted, there were advantages to this arrangement, such as our 70-year-old mother not having to push the piano to the other end of the room by herself. Also, the fact that, if it were in the family room, she might actually get a chance to see and enjoy it. But logic and convenience had nothing to do with this. This was about tradition.

Eventually, Mom got sick of our whining and promised the tree would be in the living room as usual. We all heaved a sigh of relief. Too bad none of us would be getting home at Christmas to see it.

There are few things we safeguard so closely as our family traditions. A friend of mine was appalled to discover that her new husband was a "T and A" man: tinsel and angel. She comes from a strict no-tinsel-and-a-star background. After much arguing and debate, they had to finally ask, "How important is this, really?" They bought two trees.

As my friends found out, sometimes starting a new custom is a blessed event. For the most part, I wonder at newspaper articles that encourage "Start a new Christmas tradition." To my mind, it's like enthusing "Buy your kids a large pet." Sure, it's going to be fun for the first year, but after that you're stuck with it.

Once I did try to start something new when I bought a crèche set — a miniature nativity scene. A magazine article I read suggested hiding the baby Jesus figure and then have it suddenly "appear" in the manger on Christmas Eve. I could picture this perfectly. A cozy fire crackling in the fireplace. My children standing hand-in-hand before the crèche, scrubbed and cleaned and in new pyjamas, wide-eyed with wonder to see that the manger now contained a tiny figure. What better way to show them the true meaning of Christmas?

I should have realized that it was a fantasy. I should also have realized that these articles always leave out something important (such as, if you leave the manager empty, your children will fill it with action figures, miniature animals and dead bugs). This crucial instruction was missing: "Remember where you hide the baby." Six years later and I haven't seen Jesus since I took him out of the box.

But our empty manger did teach us something: holidays are a time to share the traditions and beliefs of others. My Jewish friends suggest an empty manger means we're still waiting. My neighbour, an atheist, says he doesn't believe there ever was a figure of Jesus. A friend who works as a maternity nurse is sure Mary is just holding out until her own doctor comes on duty. As for me, I've come to see the mother before the empty crèche as an expression of my personal philosophy of the season: "I'm not ready yet."

This year is my first Christmas since my divorce, which has definitely been one of those unexpected changes. My life plan was to stay married forever. Mind you, my beauty plan was to stay 28 forever. Sometimes we're just forced to rethink. My ex-husband and I have decided that there are some holiday traditions we are going to do without this year, such as the one that says two divorced people can't be together to enjoy the day with their children just as they always have.

The truth is, what we choose to do at Christmas reflects the changes in our lives as much as the ways in which time stands still. The people we love may not always be with us. The faces around the table, as well as the tinsel and trappings, may change from year to year.

In the end, my Christmas celebration is a little like that empty manger. In the midst of life's uncertainties, it's a reminder of peace and moments of breathless anticipation. This Christmas may not look like those of my youth, but the love and hope I share may just make it feel like them. After all, some things never change.

Presence of Mind

People are always telling me that if I want to enjoy the Christmas season, I have to plan ahead. And they're right. I would be enjoying myself a whole lot more right now if I'd just taken a few moments during the year to convert to Buddhism. As it is, I'm once again getting that familiar holiday feeling: a sensation of sheer panic.

There's only one thing I need to be ready for a picture-perfect holiday. I need to have Christmas moved to February.

I suppose it's my own fault. If I didn't fritter away so much time looking after my children and trying to make a living, there would be a handmade pine-cone wreath on our door at this very moment.

This feeling of Christmas inadequacy always reminds me of a story my second-grade teacher, Miss Stewart, told about something that happened to her when she was about 20. By the time she taught me, she was closer to 108.

Early in her career, Miss Stewart moved to a new community and was honoured to be given the task of coordinating the local Christmas pageant. Her first thought was to speak to someone who had done the job before, but remarkably they had all moved to other towns. No problem. A woman who could make Dick and Jane come alive for a bunch of seven-year-olds didn't need any help with Mary and Joseph. Miss Stewart efficiently polled the community and signed up her Mary, Joseph, three wise men, angels and shepherds.

At the first rehearsal no one showed up. In fact, no amount of threatening or cajoling could get any one of them to any rehearsal at any time.

Miss Stewart rounded up another full roster of cast members. Then another. By performance time she had four full teams of actors and had not held a single rehearsal.

On pageant night the obvious happened. Every one of the actors she had recruited showed up. Hordes of wise men re-created a scene from *Exodus* down the centre aisle. A fight broke out among the angels over who would get to say the line "Peace on Earth." Miss Stewart collapsed into a seat near the back just to wait the thing out.

Then, as she told it, she was appalled to hear two elderly ladies in front of her commenting on how lovely the pageant was this year. How glad they were that there were only four Marys this year because any more led to ugly scenes as they jockeyed for position around the manger, trying to secure a spot for their baby Jesus.

Miss Stewart's moral to this story was: a person who settles for less than perfection will eventually cease to know the difference.

I see that as a good thing.

I realized years ago that from a life's wish list that includes children, perfection and sanity, you only get to pick two. So, I've come to accept that events in my house just aren't going to look like a decorator's dream. It's not a case of lowering my expectations. It's a case of no longer having any.

If anyone comments on the state of my house around the holidays, I've developed a choice of responses:

For the religiously devout: Jesus was born in a stable. I'm trying to re-create that atmosphere in my house.

For the disbeliever: I don't believe in immaculate anything.

I've also learned to welcome help. Most of the people who come for a holiday meal at my house bring part of it with them. Salespeople can also be helpful. I instruct each salesperson not to let me leave the store until I have bought a minimum of three gifts and can prove they're not for me.

Miss Stewart would never understand my acceptance of less than perfection in my holiday planning. But then, Miss

Stewart never understood why I found 1+1=2 a very limiting concept.

The truth is, there are really only two things I want from my Christmas celebration — for my family to be healthy and happy, of course, but also for me to be able to enjoy the things I do manage to do this year and not worry so much about the things I don't get to. And, who knows? If I can cut myself a little slack this year before we cut the festive turkey, this Christmas holiday just might be perfect.

January

I am starting the new year with a new philosophy of life: "That which does not kill me, makes me bitchier."

Hmm . . . you know, it's just possible that I may have a case of the January blahs.

I like the idea of having a clear, concise philosophy that sums up my approach to living. Like those ads for sports gear that carry the inspirational message "Just do it." Or, as a friend of mine prefers to say, "Just wear the clothes and pretend you did it."

In the past I have lived by such stirring phrases as "When life gives you lemons, make a vodka and tonic." Or "The best things in life are free. Except for coffee." Of course, the beginning of January is not necessarily the best time to be formulating sayings about how I see the world. Choosing a philosophy of life in the middle of winter is a little like contemplating the helpfulness of your spouse when you have guests for the weekend and PMS. It's just not going to be good.

I would like to say, in my own defence, that a little mid-winter funk is entirely warranted. In January, my city becomes the poster town for *Tundra Monthly*. Bleak, bitter, grey. Walks with the dog consist of a brisk clip to the end of the front path before he freezes to the pavement. Now and then there are a few glorious, precious moments of plus-zero weather. Then we get slush. Of course there are bright sides to January in this city. I never have to worry about driving on icy roads because the snowplow pushes a six-foot wall of snow across the bottom of my driveway and I can't get out until May.

Needless to say, this time of year, everything annoys me. Other people with winter blahs annoy me. People without winter blahs annoy me. The death sentence is too good for radio announcers who think it's cute to announce in January how many days until Christmas. This time of year just getting the day-to-day chores done is trying. There are some things we just shouldn't have to do in January. Getting out of bed would be one of them.

When you're in this January kind of bad mood there's really only one thing to do: wallow in it. There are many ways to do this. My personal favourites are: trying to return "final sale" items without the original packaging to a store; tallying up how many Air Miles I still need to collect before I can cash them all in on a box of paper clips; or reading fashion magazines.

It's not just the ads in the fashion magazines that keep me in a bad mood (although I always look for the one that says "You've come a long way, baby" so I can grouse "Well, yeah, but you're still calling me 'baby'"). It's the magazines' continual unspoken insistence that I will never be truly happy until I shrink down to a size 2, miraculously achieve the skin texture of a 12-year-old and purchase the complete line of Dior cruisewear. In January, I believe it.

This year, I decided to really revel in my annual funk. I went to an art film.

Loosely defined, an art film is any motion picture that appears to have been created with a budget of about $12 and that you have no clue what it's about. I recall the first art film I ever attended: I was the only one in the theatre toting a gallon tub of popcorn and a supersize drink. Obviously we were not here to enjoy ourselves. Art films are not simply entertainment. In fact, there is often nothing entertaining about them. This is not "art for art's sake." This is art for a purpose. One purpose is to make you feel that, because everyone around you is clearly delighted with the whole thing while you are wishing for death before the opening credits have finished rolling, they must know something you don't. Usually, I don't see the point of paying money to have a movie make me feel that way. I can get the same thing at an aerobics class. The other purpose art films fulfill is to encourage you to ask questions. The questions I usually ask are things like, "Why did I pay to see this?" and "Why is the penguin sitting in the turnip patch?"

What I find art films are most useful for, though, is nurturing my January blahs. Think the world is bleak? The filmmaker will show you that it's even worse than that. Think life is hard? Wait till you see a five-hour documentary recounting the hardships experienced by the peasant class in Siberia during the late 15th century, filmed entirely from the viewpoint of a half-eaten loaf of pumpernickel bread. An afternoon of this and a bad mood is assured right through to August.

The film I chose this time was perfect midwinter bad mood fare. It was set in Tibet. Winds howling, snow whipping — the whole thing could have been shot on location in my backyard.

The film went something like this: Sweeping panoramic view of the uppermost reaches of the Himalayan mountains, finally zooming in to show a tiny tribe of Tibetans, pluckily eking out an existence without any of the things we take for granted — like oxygen.

A lengthy segment follows in which the tribespeople are shown going about their daily routine: fixing tents, huddling over smoky fires, not finding food. The whole thing reminds me of camping. I am blissfully miserable already.

Cut to interview with chief of tribe, with translation via subtitles, discussing the spiritual beliefs and religious metaphors of the community with the film's director. Bad mood must be in excellent shape, as I find myself thinking, "He's probably actually saying, 'Hey, where'd you get that great Gore-Tex jacket?'"

Pan to director, looking concerned and wind-burned, explaining in subtitled Scandinavian that the entire economy of this community relies on the sale of salt, which they harvest annually from a faraway salt field. Men of the tribe make a 40-day trek across frozen wastelands with a team of yaks, spend two weeks gathering salt and then make the long trip back. None of the women ever go — there is a feeling that the salt field gods might not like having females around. Cut to shot of the women, none of whom seem in the least put out about this.

Next, move to scene of men sitting around smoky fire again, coughing pluckily and discussing their plans for the journey with illuminating dialogue such as, "Soon we will go to the salt field," and, "We will go to the salt field . . . soon." A lengthy discussion follows in which they try to decide how many yaks to take along — finally, remarkably, deciding on exactly the same number they've taken every year for the last 400 years.

Just when you're ready to either scream or decamp to the Schwarzenegger movie playing next door, the journey begins. Forty days of tundra and snow followed by snow and tundra. One of the yaks dies — presumably of boredom. The filmmaker captures every moment of it, right through the harvesting of the salt and the 40 days back. The best way to describe the journey back is that it looks absolutely, exactly like the trip out.

It would be hard to sum up the impact of this film in one phrase unless, of course, it was "indescribably dull." In fact, it should have been bleak enough to satisfy the most light-deprived, postholiday, middle-of-winter bad mood I could muster. Instead, I was annoyed to find that there was something in the lives of these people that didn't have the desired effect of depressing me entirely.

Life for these people was bleak and hard and monotonous — a lifetime of continuous January. And yet, they were not unhappy. The men looked forward to their travels and the rest of the tribe looked forward to, I don't know, hearing about what the snow looks like on the other side of the mountain, maybe. They rejoiced in the health of their returned yaks. They celebrated the triumph of the salt-gatherers who brought back nothing but what has been expected every year for centuries.

Perhaps the key to their obvious pleasure and content-ment is that these tribespeople are Buddhist. The basic philosophy of Buddhism is "life is suffering." Personally, I think this is a pretty astute observation for a group who probably never had to deal with a government office or try to get servicing for their VCR. I think the idea is that life is tough, so you should get over expecting anything else. Then, in those rare moments when your tent holds up in a storm or your yaks are healthy or it's possible simply for life to continue, you can say, "Hey, life wasn't tough today!" And it's a glorious moment. Like the return from the salt field.

I went home from the movie, in the comes-too-early win-ter twilight, made a fire in my fireplace and curled up for an hour with my favourite book. I cannot choose the month or the weather or the times I live in, but I can choose to see and savour the small pleasures that come to me. I am not entirely ready to give up my midwinter misery yet. But, when February finally rolls around, I may be prepared to admit that January was not quite so bleak after all.

New Year's Eve, 1999

The Y2K bug has hit our household. Every time I think about the new year, my brain shuts down.

There's no escaping talk of the millennium. The whole world will be celebrating, dancing in the streets. It's a scene that naturally leads one to think about death.

Not everybody thinks about death on New Year's Eve. Many think about it the next morning. I myself am past the age of staying out late and drinking more than is good for me. In fact, when the big moment comes at midnight, my children may think we're celebrating seeing Mom awake after 10 p.m. I find myself wishing I were a teenager again — I could make a fortune babysitting in one night.

I haven't decided how we'll mark the new year. Many people like to celebrate with family. Sometimes it helps if the family is not their own. I know families who fight constantly about when they're going to get together to show how much they love each other.

We do have a lot to make merry about. Medical science has completely changed the way we live in the 20th century. A thousand years ago life was difficult, uncertain and short. Now it's an average of 30 years longer.

I am planning some New Year's resolutions. I make a long list of resolutions every year and I'm happy to say that I keep every one of them. Usually I keep them in my bottom drawer where I won't have to look at them. What I should do is write resolutions such as "Eat more chocolate" or "Never put off till tomorrow what I can avoid doing altogether."

The New Year is also a time for reflection. Recently I watched a television program about important women in history whose accomplishments have been widely recognized (I think it was about half an hour long.) It was interesting to learn how very different women's lives were even a hundred years ago. Back then, a woman spent her days cooking, cleaning, chasing after the kids, sitting up by lamplight trying to get her work done, whereas I spend my time . . . I have electricity. There was one thing all these notable women from history had in common: they're all dead.

Death is scary. The best thing I can say about my own death is that it hasn't happened yet. I recall someone once commenting to my father, "Who really wants to live to be 100?"

Dad's answer: everyone who's 99.

But, as the saying goes, The only sure things in life are death and taxes. Whoever said that didn't have a family or he would have added "and laundry."

Even the experts can find death difficult to deal with. My friend Judith, a minister, recalls counselling a grieving family about appropriate clothing for their deceased mother. She said, "Avoid anything your mother wouldn't be caught dead in." She's still smarting.

I'd like to be cremated, but maybe that's because it's winter and I live in Canada. I'll have my ashes spread over the food court of Harrods department store in London, England. It's the only place I can imagine spending eternity. Our local airport opened a Harrods in one of the terminals, so I'll have to be careful to specify London, otherwise I'll end up spending eternity at the airport. I did that once when my flight to Newfoundland was delayed, and it's not an experience I care to repeat.

I would also like a memorial service. A memorial service is a time for people to say all the nice things about the deceased that they never said when the person was alive. I once read a 19th-century eulogy that went "The high praise given her is that she kept a clean house." I'm determined nobody's ever going to say that about me.

So far the only thing I'm reasonably sure I'll leave behind me is the bottle of salad dressing at the back of the fridge. I hope what will be found about my life is that I said "I love you" more often than I said "I want." And that I had no time to think about dying because I was far too busy living.

I don't know if that will make for a notable life. It certainly makes for a happy ending.

It's Under Control

I have just been seized by the deepest, most primeval urge known to woman. I want to do something to my hair. There should be a telephone support line I can call when I get like this — "Anne, put down the home perm and no one will get hurt."

Sometimes I trim my own bangs, which I consider the ultimate challenge — I have to find the scissors. I have a Bermuda Triangle drawer in my kitchen. I put in scissors, tape, pens, and they all disappear. Trimming my own bangs says something about who I am as a person. I'm an idiot. But I'm an optimistic idiot. Someday I will trim my bangs and not have to wear a ski hat in the house for two weeks.

I read an article once that said that Mila, former Prime Minister Brian Mulroney's wife, used to fly from Ottawa to Montreal just to get her bangs trimmed. That made perfect sense to me. Usually I entrust my hair to Kathy the Hair Goddess. In Kathy's hands my limp, lifeless hair becomes . . . cut. I used to go to another stylist, but he said a few things that bothered me, such as "Oops" and "Don't worry, it will grow back."

Kathy and I have been through some tough times together: the time I hennaed my hair green, the home perm of '98. Now I get past the home perm aisle of our drugstore by chanting, "I will look like a poodle, I will look like a poodle."

My desire to change my hair is like my need to keep a to-do list — it's a way to pretend that I'm in control of my life.

Many of us want to feel in control of our uncontrollable world. That's why we have parenting books and travel agents. We also occasionally like to feel out of control. That's why we have roller-coasters and personal relationships.

This morning I was confronted by two of the ultimate uncontrollable circumstances of life — Internet service providers and being smitten with garden statuary. Three days ago my ISP decided to "upgrade and improve service" with the result that nothing has worked since. Being without e-mail access is not exactly like having my arm cut off. It's worse. I spend long hours at the computer with nothing to do but work.

I went for a walk. I have found the secret to cut down on spending money. Don't go into stores. I did, but fortunately I bought something we really need — a plaster garden rabbit.

My husband, Michael, came home and the conversation went something like this:

> *Michael:* What's that brown thing on top of the snow pile?
> *Me:* It's a statement of my ability to impress my will on my physical surroundings.
> *Michael:* I think it just fell over.

I should be better at handling unpredictable occurrences. Years ago, in the glorious first moment of motherhood, I happily exchanged control of my life for control of my bladder. Lately my children have been turning into a parent's worst nightmare: people.

Matt announced that being a teenager means I can't make him get a haircut. I can't argue; he has photo evidence of Michael in junior high. Becky will be hitting the teen years soon, too, but we're not worried about her. My pal Lesley is going to open Lesley's Convent and we will all pay her large sums of money to put our daughters behind big walls. I asked what the girls would do there. Michael's response was, "Who cares?" I pointed out the sexism of this question and said that boys should be put there, too, but I suspect that might be defeating the purpose.

There are a few things in life I can control: my temper (although my Internet service provider would say differently) and sometimes my peace of mind (I will call Kathy instead of taking on my own hair). As for the rest of my primeval urges and uncontrollable life, well, that also includes love and wonder, dreams and desire.

Life is a roller-coaster. I will let go and enjoy the ride.

Home Alone

I've decided to quit my job. But how exactly do you resign from being a mother?

This morning Matt remembered that he needed a new book for history class — today. He can't remember the name of the book or where to buy it, but everyone else's mom got a copy three weeks ago. On sale. Then Becky announced that she has invited friends home for lunch. I remained calm: "Honey, I told you before. I need advance notice of these things."

"I know. Lunch isn't for another three hours."

Don't get me wrong. I love my kids. I just don't always love being a mother. I remember a workshop I attended many years ago entitled What Women Want. I assumed we'd be watching old Harrison Ford movies. Instead we were supposed to talk about our hopes and dreams. The woman next to me said, "All I want is to be alone in my house for an hour." At the time I thought she was insane. Now I realize she must have been a mother.

I don't expect my children to fully comprehend how much I have to do in a day. Sometimes I don't fully comprehend it myself. At the moment, my only hope for getting the laundry done is reincarnation. I do wish I could get my family to believe that I have a life apart from them, that I don't go into suspended animation when they're at school. Well, OK, some days I do, but an extra shot of coffee usually helps.

I think I adapted to parenthood fairly quickly, although I now believe that the worst possible time to have to look after a newborn is when you've just given birth. There were some difficult moments: like the time my husband, Michael, said it was much harder for him to be a new parent because he had to go to the office every day.

I bonded with my son immediately. The first time I left him with a sitter was to go on an outing to the drugstore for hemorrhoid cream. I ran all the way. The fact that the sitter had raised five children of her own in no way qualified her to look after my child for more than 10 minutes.

There were times in those early days when motherhood seemed a bit relentless. I didn't look like those mothers on TV; they had clean T-shirts. In the first few weeks I was convinced I would be at my child's high school graduation still in my housecoat. I remember going to a meeting months later thrilled that there was no baby throw-up on the front of my suit. I realized later that it was all down the back.

As my children grew older, I was able to get out more. After all, someone had to drive them to soccer and Brownies. I developed rules for dealing with the state of the house. For instance, nothing vertical ever needs to be cleaned because the dirt just falls off.

I also get to participate in exciting programs at our school. Today, for example, is Lice Check Day. The school organizers know that rooting through the hair of other people's children looking for bugs may not be a big attraction for volunteers, so they try to make it sound genteel. We are The Lice Ladies. I'm on a team with Valerie, a former nuclear engineer, and Deborah, who has a degree in marine biology. None of us would know a louse if it bit us. At one point this morning we couldn't decide if what we had found on the head of one tiny tot was a louse or just a big flake of dry scalp. We called in Debbie, the Grand Lice Lady, who proclaimed it to be a cornflake.

The truth is that motherhood is just like any other difficult, demanding job. You just never get to go home.

The day will come, I know, when my children will no longer need me every time a crisis occurs. I asked my own mother when I can expect that to happen. She says she's still waiting. But I swear, someday I will lead a totally self-indulgent life. I will own things that break. Eat food that didn't start as ground beef.

Someday my exasperating, demanding, adorable, wonderful children are going to grow up. And oh, how I'll regret it.

February

Having spent January sorting out the meaning of life, I've decided that this month, I'm up to a real challenge. I'm marking the month that brings us Valentine's Day by asking, "How do you make a romantic relationship last?" What I've finally hit on is a basic philosophy about the opposite sex that goes like this: "Men. You can't live with 'em and . . ." Well, that's about it, really.

This thought occurred to me recently as I was reading a book on relationships between men and women. The author suggested that relationships between genders are difficult because we have trouble communicating with each other. At least, I think that's what he was saying. This confirmed for me a significant piece of wisdom, which I now feel ready to share with the world: men and women are really different.

Some of the ways in which men and women are different are, of course, obvious. Men have really different underwear. I am reminded of an incident that happened when my ex-husband, Michael, and I were very newly married. I was heading off to the mall and Michael asked me if I'd pick him up a jockstrap. Uh, OK . . . no problem . . . I could do this; unembarrassed-by-icky-intimate-things-modern-woman that I am. Besides, undoubtedly Michael would be just as to delighted to help out when I asked him to buy me tampons.

Once in the store, I couldn't find men's underwear anywhere. Women's underwear is easy. Just step off the escalator and there it is, lycra, lace and "women's lacy no-nos" (as an elderly friend called them) as far as the eye could see. I finally found the men's underwear department demurely tucked into a corner behind men's hats and scarves. No athletic supports. I consulted a clerk, who asked, "Small, medium or large?"

It is the right of every bride to show off a bit. I said, "Large. I think probably large." He said, "Large is 40 to 44 inches."

There was a long pause while he waited for my response and I mused about whether I had stopped dating too soon. Finally, the clerk suggested, "It refers to waist size, madam." I bought medium.

It is not just in the obvious places that men are different, however. Our brains are different. I think this first occurred to me one afternoon years ago when I had taken my son, Matt, then aged four, to visit friends who have three small girls. The girls sat quietly on the floor playing with small toys while Matt made a climbing gym out of their couch, their armchairs, the chandelier. I think it was Dave Barry who wisely noted that "girls are just smaller versions of adults, while boys are pod people from the planet Destruct-o." Every boy I've known has gone through a phase where everything they see is either something to be whacked or something to whack it with.

Not that raising a female child is all that much easier. Women and girls are in tune with our emotions, which is what enables us to sometimes run through 20 or 30 different ones in the space of a single hour. I don't buy the myth that for one week out of four most women are insane because of our hormones. Usually, I just ignore that kind of suggestion, but there are some periods of the month when it makes me nuts.

I think the best way to understand the difference between men and women's behaviour is to picture the brain as a series of computer chips. Men are missing one chip — the one that would allow them to retain information about other people's lives.

A man hears a piece of information and his brain processes it like this: "Here is a piece of information. It has nothing to do with my life . . . or sports. I will discard this piece of information." This is not necessarily a problem unless the piece of information is something like "I need you home by 6 p.m. because I am going out," which it often is. Or, when the information is "My birthday is this Friday and let's try not to have a repeat of what happened last year." (A hint to the male reader: the right response to this kind of comment is almost never, "Why? Did I spend too much on your gift?")

This missing chip is also what accounts for a man being able to spend an entire evening playing poker with guys he's known since grade school and, the next morning, your conversation going something like this:

You: So, how does Phil like his new job?

Him: Phil has a new job?

You: Does Mike have the cast off yet?

Him: Um . . .

You: How are Dave and Kim doing with the new baby?

Him: Who's Kim?

Women's ability to retain information about people's lives is impressive. Most women I know can remember which day the kids have swimming lessons, soccer practice, choir rehearsal or the doctor's appointment that was rescheduled from the other rescheduled appointment and to take the camp health form when they go. We know where someone left their library book, their mitts, their lunch bag. We remember birthdays, anniversaries, the day we got the hamster. In fact, this chip in women's brains is so highly developed, we cannot only remember the names of Sarah Ferguson's two children, we even think we know why this is important. Men can remember who won the Master's golf tournament in 1983. The funny thing is, we both think we got a better deal.

Perhaps this chip is also what lets women see what needs to be done around a house. I heard a statistic the other day that 70 percent of all routine household chores are done by women. To tell the truth, I found this alarming. It means women are leaving 30 percent of the chores for the next week.

Another fundamental difference between men and women is the whole issue of sports. Many men like to spend large amounts of time either pushing some ball around or watching a bunch of other guys push some ball around. Many women like; well, for men not to do that.

I have to admit that in the course of my married life I was not always entirely supportive of Michael's love of sports. In retrospect, I think this was wrong of me. As was the time one spring I took his golf clubs to be regripped and, when the salesperson asked when I'd like them back, I said, "November."

After taking the time to sit down and watch a few sports programs on television, I have come to the conclusion that there is a reason why men find them so fascinating. I just still have no idea what it is. Perhaps watching sports for men is for me like going with my girlfriends to a Meg Ryan movie. You cry, you rejoice, you suffer, you hope and during the whole thing you get to eat snacks.

In the end I think it's not all that important if we understand why guys like sports. It's enough to simply accept that they do. Besides, understanding is not what makes a good relationship. A good relationship hinges on the ability to do one thing with care and sensitivity; I am speaking, of course, about gift giving.

If women do not get the importance of sports, I think it's

safe to say that men sometimes do not get the importance of gift giving. Perhaps this is because there are usually no good gifts for men. I have always thought that, if there is any truth in advertising, stores would be required to hang banners in the men's sections at Christmas or Father's Day that say: "The Perfect Gift for the Man in Your Life . . . there aren't any." The fact is, you can only buy someone so many pairs of socks or little change dishes, and most of us with a man in our lives hit that quota several Christmases ago. I have given up trying to find the perfect gift for the men I know and now try just to think of something they don't already have 12 of.

Women are easy to buy for. Just look what kind of things a woman buys herself and then buy her more of them.

In spite of this, men seem to find gift giving tricky. I think the reason for this is that, to men, a gift says "This is a gift." To a woman, it says "This is how I see you, how I feel about you, the essence of what you will always, always be in my heart." The reason we place so much importance on gifts is quite simple — we don't always have any other means of getting the information.

As a help to male readers, again let me just say that, as a general rule of thumb no woman wants to know that you look at her as a red flannel nightgown or new car mats. Weed Eaters are right out. On the other hand, contrary to everything the Victoria's Secret catalogue (and, btw, we know you're not reading this publication "for the articles") will have you believe, we also do not wish to receive tiny pieces of spandex that encourage hypothermia and have to be surgically removed from our rear ends.

Part of the problem of gift giving, I think, is that men fall prey to a lot of misinformation about what women want. Take, for example, the adage "Women value honesty." Of course, we don't, as any man who has ever honestly answered the question, "You really like my family, don't you?" will have found out.

A key to giving a woman gifts is understanding the language. A friend of mine called me on her birthday one year, sobbing that her husband hadn't given her a gift. Apparently, he'd asked her the week before what she wanted, she'd said, "Oh honey, you don't have to get me anything" and, inexplicably in the opinion of every woman we told this story to, he assumed she meant it.

To make gift giving less perplexing, I've come up with three simple guidelines for men choosing a gift for the woman in their lives:

1. The phrase "Buy the person something you'd like to get yourself" does not apply to you.

2. Nor does "It's just the thought that counts." It's also having it show up on the right day and not in the Shoppers Drug Mart bag it came in. It makes a birthday gift just that little bit more special when it's actually received sometime around your birthday. I recall a friend whose husband had a lot of trouble remembering when her birthday came. Finally, they agreed that she would remind him the week before and he'd make a reservation at some nice restaurant. That worked so well she used to remind him four or five times a year.

3. "Good things come in small packages" almost never includes drill bits.

Given how different men and women are, maybe it's not so surprising that half of all marriages end in divorce. What's amazing is that the other half don't. Even my father used to joke, "Your mother and I have had 20 happy years together which, out of 35, isn't so bad."

That you'll misjudge and misunderstand each other, at least at times and during certain sports seasons, seems to be the only guarantee you get in romantic relationships. So then, why do some just seem to work? How do you know you'll be together forever when most days you feel that, instead of a marriage licence, they should have issued you a learner's permit?

For me, there is an answer. When I can look into my partner's eyes and know that I will stay beautiful there forever. When I can be forgiven every moment of the day for being human. When I've been at my worst and found myself valued. And when we can misunderstand and misstep, make a thousand mistakes learning to be unalike and together and still love, then I will know. Then I will know. I will know then.

California Dreamin' . . . or Florida . . . Barbados would be nice . . .

This morning, I'm taking time to participate in some of the traditional activities of a Canadian winter. Whining and complaining.

Normally I'm a fairly good-natured person. I recall being

in the United States and having a cashier ask if I was Canadian because, as she said, "You've said thank you four times and I haven't even given you your change yet." But February makes me testy. If it's snowing in December, it's snowing on everyone. If it's snowing in February, it's snowing on me.

I don't have the kind of job in which I can afford to be in a bad mood. I'm a mother. Getting the kids off to school on time on a winter morning requires a fair amount of positive thinking. My priorities are not their priorities. My priorities in the morning go something like this: make lunches, yell at the kids to hurry up and get dressed, find mitts, find gym shorts, find something yellow in a lunch box and throw it out, tell Becky to find her boot, no other boot, and suggest that she go back upstairs and put on long pants because it's -30°C outside, that's why. My daughter's priority is to make a little pile of dust beside the front door. Once when my husband, Michael, was in charge of the morning rush, he came to me very concerned saying, "I think Becky is deaf. I had to tell her four times to put on her coat." Clearly, he hadn't been spending enough time with the children.

The Canadian medical establishment refuses to recognize February blahs as a serious ailment. Universal health coverage won't pay for the vital treatment I need: three weeks on a beach in Tahiti. Some health plans will pay for visits to a psychiatrist, but the worst time to visit a psychiatrist is when you're having problems. The first thing they want to do is drag out everything that's making you anxious to begin with.

What I need is a therapist who supports a coping strategy I'm good at, such as denial. A denial therapist would work something like this:

>*Me:* I'm having some problems with my mother.
>
>*DT:* Forget about it. Have a chocolate chip cookie.
>
>*Me:* I don't know where my life is going.
>
>*DT:* Clean out your closets. Maybe it will go away.

As soon as I get testy, my friends try to jolly me out of it. This has an immediate effect — I get testier. I finally called some friends and said, "I'm in a lousy, nasty mood. Come over for a chat." Strangely enough, they were all busy.

I did get to talk to a door-to-door canvasser. Icicles were forming in the beard of this nice young man and he was cautioning me about the greenhouse effect. I had to tell him that by February I start to look at the greenhouse effect as God's little gift to those of us who can't afford to go to Florida. He left me a pamphlet entitled something like Total Housecleaning with a Pine Cone and Ear Wax. I thought of inviting him in to see if he really thought that would work in my house, but anyone who gets queasy at the sight of a nuclear waste dump is not ready for my bathroom.

Dreaming of South Sea Islands doesn't help my writing either. This isn't an easy job. I remember telling Becky what I do for a living. Her lip began to tremble. "I don't want people laughing at my mother," she said. I had to be honest: "Sometimes they don't."

I should stop whining about going on vacation and think about the happiness of my family. I think my family would be happier if I went on vacation.

The tub is filling, and I have my favourite magazine. The sign on the bathroom door says "Mom On Vacation. Back To My Old Self Soon."

The Knotty Bits

The key to effective parenting is being able to provide your children with a clear, confident understanding of basic life issues that you don't have a clue about yourself.

This was brought home to me about a week ago when my son, Matt, did something totally unexpected. He asked my advice. "Mom, there's a girl at school I really like," he said, "What should I do?" I was stunned. Not because he'd asked for my opinion but because he was aware that there was a girl in his school. Even six months ago he would have said the classes were made up entirely of boys with a few misty, phantom figures in-between.

Seven years of dating and almost 20 years of marriage have taught me one or two things about male–female relationships. OK, one or two things isn't much after 27 years of study, but I've found the issue of relationships is pretty much like the issue of parenting: the more you think you know, the more you're kidding yourself.

I had just attended a parenting workshop that recommended taking a day to carefully plan your answers to the big life questions so as not to overwhelm your child. An excellent suggestion, I thought. It would give me time to make flip charts.

The next day I launched into my presentation. Matt interrupted, "Oh, I don't like her anymore."

All of this led me to reflect on the nature of true love. It also led me to reflect on the nature of parenting workshops, but that's another story.

It's not as if we hadn't broached the subject of love and sex with Matt before. As responsible parents, Michael and I had no intention of letting our son learn the facts of life on the street. We were hoping he'd pick them up from TV. Usually, we subscribe to the philosophy that you should wait to deal with the big issues until your child shows interest on his own. Mind you, if we stuck to that philosophy, neither of our children would ever have been toilet-trained.

By the time Matt was 10, he had still not asked about sex. We decided it was time. In our usual nonsexist, co-parenting attitude, we decided his father should be the one to tell him. I suggested to Michael that he get a book to help with the explanation, but he said he thought he could do it from memory.

I'm not sure what they talked about, but the discussion took 15 minutes. I was astonished. I wouldn't have had enough material for 10. Later Michael reported that Matt had shown no interest in the topic whatsoever. I couldn't decide if that was the reaction we wanted or not.

> *Me:* How did you work in the idea of respect?
> *Michael:* I didn't use the words babe or score.
> *Me:* Did you explain to him about the wonder and mystery of male–female relationships?

Michael: I told him it had always been a mystery to me.

Sex and relationships weren't discussed much when I was young. I remember my older sister, Keltie, bursting into my room in excitement the night before her wedding to say that our mother had just given her The Talk. Keltie said that Mom had got most of it right. My own relationship education was limited to Keltie's warning me before my first date that I should leave my ski jacket on during the movie. I didn't understand why I should do this but I remember marvelling that people could date right through August.

When Matt asks about love again, I will tell him that love is about passion, yes, but also about trust, support, communication and responsibility. Also I want it to sound like fun. I will explain the difference between love and sex and why I hope he will find only relationships where there is no difference at all.

When it comes right down to it, there is only one thing I can tell my son about love that is absolutely clear and straightforward. Love falls into two categories: devastating and heartbreaking, and glorious and ecstatic. And the only guarantee is that you're going to get both.

Because the truth of the matter is that the best things in life are free. But they're never simple.

Spring

March

Today, I would like to explore the topic of uncertainty. I'm just not sure how to go about it.

There are many great joys of being a writer. The writing part is not generally one of them. Someone once said, "Creativity is a struggle achieved laboriously against overwhelming odds." Personally, I think that's being optimistic. Writing consists of long periods of time spent alone, staring at a blank page or computer screen, praying for either inspiration or a job with a health plan at IBM.

Today is not a day to be inside trying to write. Spring is creeping around the edges of winter this morning; a warm whisper of air from the south suggests that the frost and chill might not last forever. It feels almost time to start doing spring things. There is an old adage that goes "When the weather turns nice, it's time to clean your house." I massage it a little to say "When the weather turns nice, it's time to sit on your deck." I've never understood the wisdom of celebrating the first few warm days of spring by holing up inside, scraping scum off the kitchen sink.

The kids can smell spring in the air and start to spend more time in our tiny inner-city backyard. I have to remind them to go inside now and then to get some fresh air. Where I live, spring is a joyous, magical season that lasts about fifteen seconds. Last year I missed it entirely because I went to the bathroom.

Of course, it's not really spring yet. We'll be well into April before the snow in my backyard finally dissolves into mud. Mud is the afterbirth of spring. For now, March brings promises and warm breezes one day, icestorms the next. March is a good month to contemplate the idea of uncertainty. My friend Ina tells me that, growing up in Poland, they used to call March the "stew pot" month; it was a mixture of everything. Ina says all of the months had names to identify their nature. This makes great sense to me. Where I live, January would be called the month of "Well, it can't get any colder than this." February, the month of "We were so wrong," March, "We complained about cold? Slush is worse!" June, the month of "My God, the heat . . ." right on to October, "What? Snow, already?"

At least we'd know what to expect. In actual fact, of course, March is named after Mars — the god of war — recognition, I suppose of the clashing elements and uncertain nature of the month.

I have to say that I don't enjoy uncertainty. It makes me feel very . . . I don't know . . . uncertain. I'm not alone in this feeling; that's why a lot of people spend a lot of time and energy trying to assure us of what the future holds. Depending on how much they charge an hour, these people are called either financial analysts or telephone psychics.

Realistically, I don't believe you can tell the future by reading tea leaves or consulting a palmist. I had a tarot reader once who told me that all that stuff is bunk. When it comes to my financial future, though, I do wish I could have some degree of certainty. So far, I have a long-term investment plan, which I refer to as "Matt and Becky." And I have a retirement plan. I plan never to retire.

This time of year, I'm recovering from the annual bombardment of advertising by investment companies, urging me to be responsible with my savings. I have to admit, I have occasionally been known to invest all of my spare cash in the women's shoe industry. The prudent thing to do, the financial professionals assure me, is to give it to a group of people I've never met who will use it to bankroll business speculations that I don't understand. At least with the shoes, I know what I'm getting into.

There are good reasons for wanting to know where you're going and how you're going to get there. And not just so that you can start complaining about it well in advance.

A friend of mine argued for months with her husband about whether to find out the sex of their third child before it was born. They had two children in late elementary school and my friend contended that this baby had already been surprise enough for her. Her husband said that knowing the sex in advance would take all the fun out of the birth. Yes . . . of course . . . that really great time she would otherwise be having . . . Anyway, eventually they agreed that she would find out, but she promised not to tell him and, I have to say, she was as good as her word. Of course, it would have been even better if she hadn't immediately painted the nursery pink.

I will be the first to admit that working as a freelance writer is not a perfect arrangement for someone who dislikes uncertainty. On the one hand, I can't say enough good things about my boss, but on the other, the anxiety caused by uncertainty can be pretty extreme. As a freelancer, knowing what my workload was going to be like in advance would allow me to do some important things. Like sleep and eat.

Still, I continue to try to feel in control of my future. I run through the rain to buy the newspaper so I can read about what the weather is going to be like. I recall reading somewhere that ancient man (I'm pretty sure it wasn't ancient woman) dragged the boulders of Stonehenge together to create a kind of giant calendar, allowing him to forecast seasonal changes for the first time in history. You could just see how it would be very effective. "Yup, there's snow on the rocks, must be winter."

It's not just the future that's unpredictable; some days I feel I can't even be certain of the present. These days, even my role as a mother seems uncertain. As a child, I knew exactly what my father was supposed to do: go to work, take us fun places and remove dead rodents. I also knew what my mother was supposed to do: everything else. I now find myself trying to support a family like my father did while, at the same time, struggling to raise my children and keep house exactly like my mother did. I don't need more role models — I need fewer.

Gender roles, in general, seem to be more uncertain these days. I recall the day a few years ago that two young gay men moved onto our street. Neighbours collected on front lawns, staring with disbelief at the French antiques and floral upholstered wingbacks being carried into the house. "Well, you know what this means," one of the husbands shook his head in distress. "Our lawns will never look as good as theirs."

Whatever the misgivings, this couple contributes a lot to the quality of life on our street, particularly on neighbourhood garage-sale day. The stuff they get rid of is always twice as nice as the stuff the rest of us are keeping.

My friend Avi, who is also a gay man, pushes me to accept that nothing in life is black or white; everything is rainbow. Avi's way of being in the world challenges my assumptions about roles and role models. For instance, where I come from, a person like Avi, whose name begins with "doctor" and who is a pillar of his religious community, does not come wafting blithely into rooms with an aura that announces, "I am here, and I'm wearing purple!" Avi's willingness to push the boundaries of what's accepted makes me think there is truth in the saying that "Being normal is not necessarily a virtue. It rather denotes a lack of courage." Through his eyes, it's possible to see that giving up certainty about how things should be is, perhaps, a small price to pay for being able to explore all the shades and colours and possibilities of life and of yourself.

In a few weeks, Avi and I will take our annual spring ramble through the civic gardens and he will tell me again that Mother Nature created gay men so that there would be someone who could fully appreciate her colour schemes. When I wonder about what is certain in sexual roles today, I always end up feeling sure of one thing: love is too rare a gift to quibble about what gender it comes in. And perhaps being confused is not such a bad thing; at least it means I'm still thinking.

In the end, the truth might be that the only thing I can ever know for certain is that I may never be certain at all — not of my future, not even, perhaps, of my role or opinions in the present. But then, after all, this is March. March is not a time for certainty. Nature will push itself into birth this month, but not without struggle and strain, clash and contradiction. For this moment in time, nothing is certain. Which means anything is possible.

Grey Expectations

I'm beginning to think I've hit pre-premenopause. There's a technical term for this stage of life: it's called denial.

I'm not sure why I suddenly feel older. I turned 44 this year, but that's not yet middle age. Middle age is five years older than whatever age I am. My hair is starting to grey, but that began around the time my daughter started picking out her own clothes. And I do get hot flashes, but only when I think of my to-do list for tomorrow.

I think awareness of aging has come with the realization that I will buy anything from a salesperson who calls me Miss and that if a construction worker whistles, it means there's a teenage girl walking behind me.

I know I can't stop the march of time; I just wish it wasn't using my face as the main parade route. At the point when life is supposed to be getting less complicated, I'm now using a 627-part skin-care system.

My husband, Michael, is not always a lot of help. When I complain that I look haggard and drawn he says, "Honey, you look the same to me."

I've decided it's time to resort to drastic measures: I've joined a gym.

I'm not really a gym person. I knew it from the moment I signed up for the fitness assessment test.

"What do you mean, I can't drink coffee before the test?"

"Coffee pumps up your heart rate. We want to test you in your natural state."

That is my natural state.

Next I completed the fitness profile form.

1. Current fitness strategy: Avoidance. I have a 100 percent success rate.
2. Reason for choosing our gym: Proximity to a doughnut shop.

3. Area that most needs attention: Public funding for daycare.

My fitness profile came back reading "Should not use the change room without medical supervision."

I have to admit there are advantages to getting older. My children, Matt and Becky, are becoming more independent every year. There are occasions when the need for love and attention is still huge, but I'm sure I'll grow out of that in time.

I've also acquired a certain amount of wisdom. A younger friend of mine is expecting her first child, and I have a wealth of knowledge to share with her. As she frets about whether to hire a midwife or just hope that her own doctor will be available for the delivery, I'm dying to assure her that when the baby is ready to be born, she won't care if the janitor delivers it. Of course, the other side of experience is knowing that there's such a thing as knowing too much.

What I really need at this point is to talk to an older woman about what life brings as we age and slow down. My mother has just passed her 70th birthday, and I would like to talk to her about it, but I can't — she's away skiing. In summer she plays tennis three times a week. A few years ago she finished a Master's degree and was ordained a minister. She now works part-time at a church, running a program for new mothers and visiting "the elderly."

We keep waiting for signs that Mom is slowing down. Sure enough, last week Mom called complaining of a few aches and pains. I was gentle, "Well, you're getting on."

"You're right," Mom sighed, "I should warm up before I go snowboarding."

If I'm feeling older, maybe it's because I've reached one of the ultimate milestones of maturity: the realization that I have something to learn from my mother. It reminds me of coming home from my first year at university and being amazed at how much my parents had matured.

I'll be lucky to have my mother's energy when I'm 70. I'd be lucky to have my mother's energy now. When the fitness form asked for Person to Contact in Case of Emergency, I should have put "my mother." She'll probably be on the exercise bike next to me.

If I'm not snowboarding when I'm 70, frankly, I'll be relieved. What I do hope is that I'll share my mother's enthusiastic approach to the future. I'm embracing this next stage of my life with the aid of some traditional wisdom: youth may be fleeting, but the possibilities of life are endless.

The Goddess Within

Today I am going to reveal to my daughter, Becky, the wonder and majesty of the Goddess in Womanhood. Just as soon as I finish waxing my legs and flea-dipping the dog.

Ordinarily, "goddess" is not a concept that interests me much. As my friend Patty notes, nowadays sacrifices are rarely made to the goddess — they're made by her. But lately I've been stirred by the magic of spring and the realization that life goes in circles. I'm once again at a time in my life when clothes matter. The bag has to match the shoes, which have to match the outfit — I mean my daughter's bag, shoes and outfit, of course. The last time I bought something hot and trendy it was a cappuccino.

As I move through my forties, I am struggling to come to terms graciously with the process of aging. It can be a little daunting at times. If your face is your fortune, I have clearly become a victim of recession. Just this morning, I went to wipe mascara out from under my eyes and realized I wasn't wearing mascara. At the same time, Becky is just entering womanhood, and I have a vast store of wisdom and experience to share with her — if only I knew how to do it. Too many young girls end up "looking for love in all the wrong places" like, say, *Cosmopolitan* or *Teen* magazine.

Many women's magazines are criticized for obsessing solely about unrealistic body images. This is not true. They also obsess about unrealistic sex — how to do it, when to do it, with whom to do it. In my life that kind of list usually refers to a car pool. These articles make it clear that a fulfilling sex life takes the participation of two people — me and the writer of the article. From what I gather, the guy doesn't have to do anything.

The magazines I recently looked at had articles such as "New Tactics in the Bedroom." That made me feel as if I'd be having a romantic interlude with GI Joe. Another was titled "Under the Covers: Keeping Him Guessing." Maybe I'm missing something here, but in my experience, once you're under the covers, the guessing part is over. My favourite was "What He Thinks When He Sees You Naked." As a friend of mine observed, "In our house that would be, I thought it was my day to get the shower first."

I recall once being invited to a home party entitled Rekindling Romance: A Sampling of Marital Aids. I had always thought a marital aid was a decent night's sleep or a reliable babysitter. The evening was a real education. I had no idea underwear could be considered a food group or that romance required four AA batteries. I pictured myself at the crucial moment saying, "Just a minute, I think the ones in Big Bird's Talking Schoolbus might still be OK." The woman sitting next to me said wistfully, "My husband's no Energizer Bunny."

It's time to talk to Becky about the changes her body will be going through soon. I remember getting my first training bra. I didn't have a clue what I was supposed to be training "them" to do. Our gym teacher provided girls with many detailed pamphlets on menstruation. At the moment it finally occurred, I could have written a Ph.D. thesis on what was happening to my body. I just had no idea what to do about it. A girl from the tough crowd took me aside and gave me a graphic explanation of personal care. I am still grateful.

When Becky begins to menstruate, I would like to throw my own home party. I'll invite women and girls of all ages. We'll share stories of what life has taught us. Maybe I'll put flowers in my daughter's hair and my own. For a few more precious moments, my opinion will mean as much to her as that of the unknown writers at *Seventeen* magazine. Before they suggest that her body is anything but perfect or that sex is a tool rather than a gift, perhaps I'll be able to convince her to celebrate her womanhood — at every stage of life. Then, if the world does not show her the beauty and wisdom of the goddess within herself, my daughter will know exactly where to look.

Expert Advice

I've finally found a productive use for my chaotic, confusing life. I'm going to write a self-help book.

The idea came to me while I was taping a segment of "HineSight" for *Canadian Living Television*. It's a weekly minute-and-a-half where people get to see me cleaning out my fridge, scraping soap scum off the bathtub — all the things you really want to be seen doing on national television.

At first television rattled me. I had a lot of trouble getting into character, which is scary because I'm playing myself. My producer would say things like, "Anne, would you really wear a ratty sweatshirt to clean the floor?" Ordinarily I'd wear my afternoon tea gown, but it's on loan to the Queen. Eventually I came to enjoy doing television — partly because it provides video evidence of me cleaning the house (believe me, there's no other proof), but also because being on television means instant authority. It no longer matters that I can't get my family to listen to what I tell them; I am now qualified to give advice to total strangers.

I've bought several excellent self-help books myself over the years. I have one on time management that I haven't had a chance to read yet. I'm going to read *Getting Organized* just as soon as I can find where I put it.

The advantage of self-help books is the expert advice. It's usually the same advice my mother gives me, but the authors never finish off by saying "If you'd sat up straight at the dinner table, this wouldn't be happening." It makes all the difference. These writers really know their topics. I saw a writer on television talking about his book on successful marriages, which he knows a lot about because he's had four.

My local bookstore has stacks of useful books. There is *The Art of Everyday Ecstasy*, which I think must be about finally getting the laundry done, and *The Nine Fantasies That Will Ruin Your Life*, which must be about thinking I ever will get the laundry done. There was one called *The Highly Sensitive Person*, which I found insulting, and another one called *What to Say When You Talk to Yourself*. I can only assume it's "What, are you crazy?"

I almost bought *Awakening Intuition* but I had a hunch I wouldn't like it.

I think I will write a motivational self-help book. It will give me something to do when I'm avoiding work. The key, of course, is to think of a subject about which I have some expertise. Maybe *101 Places to Hide Small Appliances You're Embarrassed You Bought*.

I could write about how to avoid boredom in a long-term relationship. My advice: If you want to keep a warm feeling all over and a flutter in your heart, drink coffee.

I could also write a book for working mothers: *You Can Have It All, You Just Can't Sleep*. Chapter 1: "Cutting Out the Inessentials: Wean Your Family Off Food."

One self-help book that I bought when I was working outside the home is filled with inspirational examples of how other women run their lives much better than I do. My favourite section is "Finding the scissors: If your scissors are continually lost, save time by labeling the scissors with which drawer they go in, labeling the drawer, compiling a list of activities for which the scissors can be used . . ." By that time I could have found the scissors, even in my house.

Expert advice can be wonderful. If mothers of several small children were advising heads of state, the world would be a more peaceful place. But self-help books can do as much to make me feel less perfect as more perfect. So instead of reading or writing a book to understand life, maybe I'll take a radical course and just try to live.

I may not ever be perfectly organized, a perfect parent or a perfect partner, but I have a bigger dream for myself — maybe, just maybe, I'll be content.

April

I am designating April the month of "I wanna go somewhere!"

The world is waking up and I'm suddenly feeling as restless as the first spring breeze. I can sense the energy in the ground as I turn over earth in the garden, can feel a surge of life in the trees around me, ready to burst into leaves. I want to go somewhere where spring is already blooming, the world feels new and the city signs say, "Paris."

Travelling was a big part of our family life when I was growing up. Almost every summer my parents packed us up and took us off on a family trip — coast to coast, even overseas. It must have been incredibly stressful to travel with five kids, though, as Mom says, "Not as stressful as staying home with five kids."

Travelling as a family gave us a chance to see parts of countries that other tourists miss. Mostly hospital emergency wards. My brother David could write a travel book on "The ten worst countries in which to have an allergic reaction to food." I think the former Soviet Union topped the list. We had David's head stitched up in British Columbia and my baby sister Kathryn's thumb tip sewn on in Bermuda (every time a kid slams a door in my house now, they moan, "I know, Mom, you're going to tell us what happened to Aunt Kathryn" . . . and I do). And my older brother Bruce almost had to have his finger surgically removed from a display case he was fiddling with in Robbie Burns' Scottish home.

While my mother loved to travel, it made my father nervous. In retrospect, this was understandable. Other than knowing there would be at least one outing to the local hospital, travelling with our family had its share of surprises. On a trip to Bermuda, when I was 10 or 11, we were all given tourist cards to fill out on the plane. At the airport customs station, the officer went through our cards with crisp, British efficiency. "Which one is Bruce?" My father pointed. "And Keltie?" Dad indicated my older sister. "And which one," the official peered coolly over his glasses, ". . . is Venus Aphrodite?" There was a pause during which my father turned 17 shades of purple and then sputtered, "Aaaaaaaaanne!" How did he know? We were studying Greek and Roman gods in school and, frankly, I did not come a thousand miles away from home to an exotic island to be just "Anne."

There is no doubt that travel can transform you, but it could get a little confusing at times. I had to try to remember, for example, that my sister Keltie was 16 if she met older teenage guys, 14 if she met younger teenage guys and 12 when we went for the "children eat free" buffet at the dining room.

For my mother, what made all of this worthwhile is her love of adventure. She has roamed the courtyards of Florence, cruised fjords in Norway and walked on the Great Wall of China. My mother also loves to shop. We used to say that when she and my sister Kathryn visited a foreign country it was considered a local economic initiative plan. I have an elderly aunt who also shops the world, but never declares anything. I've met her coming off planes, shouldering Persian carpets or buried under armloads of Chinese silks, announcing, "No, no, nothing to declare," and they wave her through. I was once raked over the coals for not disclosing a half-eaten sandwich I'd forgotten in my carry-on. When I suggest to my aunt that it would be wise to come clean to Customs, she says that she has no intention of telling a perfect stranger what she bought on her trip.

I have certainly inherited a love of faraway places. I don't care if I'm looking at rocks and scrub bush, it's all exotic because it's foreign rocks and scrub brush. The two essential luxuries of life seem to me to be a truly comfortable bed and travel. Unfortunately, you rarely get both together.

The more I get to travel, the more I am filled with wonder.

For instance, it is a wonder to me that there are still places in the world where they will agree to rent me a car. When I travel, I try to leave behind all of the things I will never use, like maps. Consequently, I often end up driving on things that are not really technically considered roads. It is not easy to drive "off road" in rental vehicles, which are usually barely up to "on road." I am convinced, for example, that "Hyundai" is Korean for "not really a car."

Of course, in some places, off road is the only really safe place to be. I have driven in many, many places where what was considered a proper road, was certainly not. In Hampshire in England, for example, someone came up with the ingenious idea of transforming narrow ox-cart paths into modern roadways by simply drawing a white line down the middle. As a foreigner, I found myself driving on the wrong side, shifting gears with the wrong hand as the other cars came hurtling toward me, barrelling by so close I could tell you the colour of the other driver's eyes and threatening to send me careening off into the hedgerows. I became very attached to the little car I drove there; they practically had to pry my fingers off the steering wheel.

Driving in Montreal is also a hair-raising experience. No wonder they have so much more joie de vivre there; they know they might die at any time trying to make the left turn at Peel and Sherbrooke. The definition of "parking lot" in Montreal is "any paved surface." I was in that city once during a strike of the public transit workers and people were parking their cars on sidewalks, in front of driveways. A week later the buses started running again and nothing changed.

It is absolutely true that travel is a broadening experience. I couldn't do up my jeans for a month after my last trip. Paris, my favourite city in the world, is truly the "city of romance"; I fell in love with a different bakery on every corner.

Sampling the local fare is one of the great adventures of travel. In Newfoundland, I tried a local delicacy charmingly named "cod's tongues." I asked my waitress what they really were as I happily chowed down on a big plateful and, of course, they are cod's tongues. In Denmark, I could not get used to having an assortment of luncheon meat on my plate each morning. The day I cooked a "real" breakfast for my hosts, they were appalled; eggs and bacon are for dinner. Switzerland is a good country; they eat chocolate for breakfast. In Tennessee I sampled a local food that I called "See how much cholesterol you can get on a plate." They called it "grits," which is a cornmeal mush smothered in butter or chicken gravy or both. It's delicious.

A Japanese friend who visited once could not believe what North Americans were prepared to eat. Akiko would sit munching her breakfast of boiled tofu and sea urchins, and assure me that peanut butter and jam on bread was simply weird.

Remembering the tastes and sights of my travels makes me long to be going somewhere. In order to travel overseas, however, I constantly have to confront my most basic fear: becoming poor. Travel is expensive. There are books available that tell you how to backpack and camp across Europe but, to my mind, they may as well be titled "Sleeping with a rock in your back in seventeen different countries."

Of course, comfort has its price. A friend of mine tells the story of being in the French countryside with his family and suddenly coming upon a spectacular and ancient castle that had been renovated into a luxury hotel. As Dave tells it, they decided to stay, and they spent the afternoon roaming the magnificent grounds, feasting that evening in the sumptuous dining room. The next morning, Dave went to pay the bill: "I didn't care if one night for five people cost, say, even eight hundred dollars. This was a once-in-a-lifetime hotel stay." The bill was $10,000. I asked Dave about his reaction. "I'm not sure," he says, "I blacked out." But, he does say he learned a valuable lesson from this experience, "It's really, really hard to cash in a North American retirement policy from France."

I will not be going to that hotel anytime soon. In fact, unless the cherry tree outside my workroom window miraculously starts dropping $5 bills instead of petals, the only trip on my horizon is to our local "No Thrills" grocery store. The only mountain to be tackled is the laundry in the basement.

Somewhere in the world there are thousand-year-old temples and breathtaking fjords and sidewalk cafés. Somewhere only those who live there need to work and clean and chase after the children, while those who visit can stroll and wonder and dream.

Perhaps, if I leave my work for an hour, go outside beyond the small concerns of my day, I can enjoy the newness in the earth beneath my feet, if not in the sights around me. Perhaps the air will smell like London in the morning and the new flowers remind me of gardens in

France. Well, probably not. For now, I will have to live with my restlessness. If I want to listen to a foreign language I can talk to my teenage son. And if I want unusual food, I can actually cook dinner. Someday, I will go again. I will head out across the prairies after the buffalo or into a small boat bound for a new world. Today, I will try to savour what is wondrous in my own backyard. And dream of Paris.

Chatelaine billed this piece
Survivor: The Kitchen Island Edition

I am an amazing cook. When I actually cook something, everyone is amazed. Slaving over dinner means I have to find the scissors before I can open the package. So, when *Chatelaine* asked me to write a piece about serving nothing but home-cooked made-from-scratch meals for a week, I was delighted. They were sending me a chef! No, it turned out that the idea was that I would cook all of our meals and snacks from scratch.

Hmm. I know what scratch is: any product that has fewer than three ingredients and does not come tinned or packaged. I didn't like the sound of this. It might seriously affect the well-being of my family. Could I still have coffee? Yes, coffee would be OK. What about pasta? Only if I buy the ingredients and make the noodles myself. In other words, no pasta.

I do have some experience in cooking like my foremothers. A power outage once forced me to make cappuccino on a gas barbecue. OK, it's possible my foremothers were more concerned about not being eaten by wolves than trying to get the milk frothy, but I'm sure it's the same principle.

I've often regretted that I don't serve my family homemade meals like the ones my mother served. I frequently use packaged and ready-made foods. Let's face it, if the four food groups were fat, sugar, salt and propylene glycol alginate, we'd be eating wonderfully well-balanced meals. But cooking nutritious home-cooked meals takes time. Buying quality convenience food takes money. I don't always have a lot of either.

Food is a precious gift — maybe cooking from scratch for a week will give me a renewed appreciation of it. Besides, this project speaks directly to the words by which I have always lived my life: "Never turn down work."

One week to go: Break the news to the kids

Have made a deal with my editor: we are allowed one luxury item each. Tell the kids this is just like *Survivor*. My son, Matt, says, "Why? Are we going to have to eat bugs?" I lecture the children on the importance of getting into the spirit. Perhaps we will all wear sarongs.

Matt chooses Nestea. (I don't give my kids pop because it gives them a sugar high. I give them iced tea, which, of course, gives them a caffeine high.) My daughter, Becky, chooses KFC popcorn chicken. The "meal deal" comes with a drink, fries and a treat. She's afraid of what might otherwise end up in her lunch box.

Key to this assignment is to plan ahead. Unfortunately, it takes me several days to realize that. Hours before I have to make first from-scratch meal, I start to think about what I can cook. Recipes I normally use call for items such as tinned tomatoes and soy sauce. Realize that to do this assignment, will have to purchase things I'll never have use for again. Like flour. And a cookbook.

Mother loans me cookbook from 1947. From days when men were men and women cooked things such as pork hocks. First recipe I flip to is Squirrel Pot Pie ("Procure six grey squirrels"). Figure you can't get any more "scratch" than that. Foreword to book asserts that all relationship problems can be solved by woman of the house putting attractive, nutritionally complete meal on dinner table each evening. Who knew? Cancel all future sessions with therapist and head to grocery store.

Sunday dinner: Plug in the pressure cooker

Decide to start simple: barbecued meat, steamed veggies and rice. Wait — cannot use barbecue sauce. No problem; will whip some up. Read ingredients on bottle. Water, sugar, tomato paste — cannot use tomato paste. No problem; will whip some up. Discover tomato paste is not made by throwing soggy tomatoes in blender and letting it run on high for a while. Sadly, cannot find monosodium glutamate among aged spice bottles in cupboard. Add everything else I do have to the blender mixture. Find that sum of all ingredients listed on label is not equal to anything resembling barbecue sauce. Dinner is late. Toss salt and pepper on meat and slap on barbecue.

Matt, Becky and I discuss how this is already turning into an educational experience. Just tonight they expanded their vocabularies to include "unpalatable" and "bland."

Cookbook author assures me that children are delighted with dessert of fresh fruit, attractively arranged. Realize she and I may live in same world, but we do not inhabit same universe.

Afterward, spend three hours making bread for the week. Starting to feel like a real homesteader. Might start wearing skirts. Recipe calls for six billion cups of flour and oceans of salt and buttermilk. It produces two small lumpy loaves. Discover there is a real difference between price of buying bread and making it yourself — these loaves cost about $4 each. Matt eats one as a snack. I am hysterical. Flour and sugar all over floor. Dog is delighted.

Monday: Jellied tuna and fossilized apples

Mom calls and suggests dropping by for lunch. Cookbook author thinks Jellied Tuna Loaf is perfect luncheon food. Suggest to Mom that we try next week.

Time to make treats for kids. Call friend Liz to get her grandmother's shortbread recipe. Basically, it's 10 parts butter to 20 parts icing sugar. Most ends up on floor again. Afraid dog is going to be diabetic by end of week. Mix dough and taste — a few times. Sometime later, put remaining dough into oven. Kids want to know why recipe made four cookies. Send Matt to store for sugar and make another batch. Kids won't eat them. Sarah from next door eats eight. I love Sarah.

Decide to make taffy apples next because I don't like them. Take more than an hour to make six of these goodies but they are perfect: traditional treat, handcrafted with painstaking care and attention. Becky eats half of one and says she's finished. Find self insisting she finish all her high-calorie, massively sugared snack. Am losing it. Remaining taffy apples permanently adhered to plate. Neighbour Cheryl suggests it is now art. Sarah is happy to eat them. I love Sarah.

Tuesday: Homesteading is for wimps

Have abandoned 1947 cookbook for the *Chatelaine Cookbook* from 1965. Read in introduction that I am "busy careerist." This sounds better. Foreword suggests that busy careerist, before leaving for downtown with husband, takes five minutes to roll wet pot roast in dry onion-soup mix, place in foil, then seal it airtight and set in the oven. "With the automatic timer set . . . she steps out confidently, knowing there is a delicious meat course ready at 5:30 p.m."

Of course, she's forgotten to pack lunches, find gym shorts and get kids to daycare. Obviously, times have changed from when a woman worried about dinner before she and her husband both drove off to work together. Today they'd take separate cars.

Knock off work an hour early to start cooking fudge for kids' snack and chicken pot pie for dinner in time to take Becky to tutoring and pick up Matt from basketball practice. Remind myself that foremothers never had to get home-steading children to homesteading karate class or soccer games. So what if they had to deal with wolves; at least wolves came right to door. Starting to wonder if I can do this.

Wednesday: Mutiny without bounty

Am tired of eating lumpy bread and boiled eggs for lunch. Friend calls from British Columbia, upset that she almost hit deer with van. My first thought: "A deer is a single-ingredient item — I could cook that!" This is not normal.

Matt calls wondering why I am a half-hour late to pick him up from computer lessons. Suddenly figure out how to keep up with cooking and deal with kids' activities at same time. Call and cancel all of kids' activities.

Decide there is only one way to deal with this misery — share it with friends. Invite people for dinner Friday night.

6 p.m.: Slipped at dinner tonight: used seven drops of Tabasco in hamburgers. Feel like I should go to confession. Find only way to get dinner made and still have time for work, laundry and housekeeping is to resort to extreme and unusual measures, such as asking kids to help.

Realize I have not chosen my own luxury item for week. Try to decide between chocolate, on the extreme off-chance that I feel like eating some soon, or wine, which I can serve on Friday evening. No contest. I'll just make wine. Reflect on fact that, as a rule, generally, wine is aged longer than two days. Reluctantly, must sacrifice personal happiness for safety of guests.

8 p.m.: Must make more bread. Find recipe that uses three cups of plain yogurt. Excellent. It's fast and easy. Only downside? Bread is inedible. Sarah thinks it's delicious. Plan to adopt Sarah.

Go back to regular yeast recipe. Will triple it so there will be enough bread to last for rest of week. Sometime later, Matt wanders into living room — where I am planning dinner party menu and wondering if trying to make my own bouillon cubes is sure route to insanity — and asks what that blob is that's taking over kitchen. Lava flow of dough has swelled over side of bowl, completely engulfing countertop.

11 p.m.: Crouched on floor over kitchen pail, kneading 600 tons of bread dough and fending off dog. Swear never to put "pioneer" on list of potential career options. Try making apple pie at same time and end up forgetting sugar. Discover that anyone who says you can't add sugar after the crust is on and pie has been in oven for 40 minutes just isn't trying. Remember that my chosen luxury item is wine. Consider this very good planning.

Thursday: Tidy-up time

Kids are sick of eating lumpy toast and boiled eggs for breakfast. Dinner party is tomorrow night. Realize that, on top of cooking, have to clean house. There is flour and sugar in every crack and crevice of kitchen. Draw up schedule for day of party that does not allow for leisure activities such as showering or going to bathroom.

Friday: D for dinner party

Abandon any pretense of doing job. Shop, cook, clean. Friend Liz arrives early to help out. How did she know? Bless ex-husband who arrives to take kids to dinner so I will not have to cook for them too. Wonder if he did it for my benefit or theirs. Suddenly realize that tomorrow is Saturday and kids will expect to eat again. Will introduce them to classic made-from-scratch fare known as leftovers.

Friends arrive promptly at 7 p.m. They all bring food. Do not consider this a vote of confidence. Tell them exactly what they can do with their food: leave it so I can eat it the moment this assignment is done.

Sunday: Deep-dish thoughts

Reflect on what this week has meant. First, have found that it is possible to cook entirely from scratch, keep a job and look after a family. Just not at the same time. Tomorrow, the chips, the packaged cereal and the store-bought baking will be back on my shelf. Food is a precious gift, but so are time and sanity. Cooking from scratch for a week has given me a new appreciation of both. And, after all, there are many things that feed a family. So, this afternoon I'm going to play gin rummy with Becky, help Matt with his homework and spend a whole half-hour alone with a good book and a cup of tea. For dinner, we're ordering pizza with everything . . . except regrets.

A Matter of Opinion

You know, I think I have hit on one of the great truths of life. Other people are strange.

This thought occurred to me recently as I was attending a wedding. Weddings themselves are not strange; the people having them sometimes are. It's no wonder. Somewhere, someone decided that the happiest day of your life is the one when you are most likely to develop an anxiety-related rash. I think the happiest day of mine was when I decided to stop vacuuming under the beds.

At this particular wedding the minister read a lovely passage of scripture: "To everything there is a season, and a time to every purpose under the heaven." I thought, "What a wonderful sentiment. Time for everything. Whoever said that obviously didn't have kids."

To tell the truth, when my children were young I discovered I could make time for most things if I just kept in mind what things could be put off for a little while. So far I've been putting off using the bathroom for 13 years. I look forward to a bright day in the future when scientists will be able to selectively breed mothers to not have personal needs.

Hearing this piece of scripture made me recall the moment I first realized that other people don't see the world the way I do. Years ago I had a summer job on Prince Edward Island. I loved the Island but at first I had a lot of trouble going without some of the things I had been used to in the city. Like stress.

Across the road from where I worked lived an elderly gentleman who ruled the town from an aluminum chair in his front yard. He had a keen interest in everything that went on at our Island theatre, short of being persuaded to actually attend a performance. One day he called me over and said, "Now, you're from Toronto, aren't you?"

"Yes," I said.

"A lot of people live in Toronto," he said.

"Yes," I said.

He looked down the potholed dirt road, past the wharves and out to the fishing boats bobbing in the afternoon tide and asked, "Now what do you suppose all those people want to live so far away from everything for?"

I realized at that moment that two people in the same place at the same time can see the world in completely different ways — a good lesson to learn because shortly after that I got married. I suggested to my husband, Michael, that perhaps we could cut down on some of our weekend activities that didn't contribute to our quality of life. Michael agreed, noting that it would give us more time for activities that did contribute to our quality of life. The funny thing is, we were both talking about golf.

I try to keep an open mind about the fact that other people have different viewpoints than I do. I try to accept that when my bank closes our local branch and I have to travel through three time zones to the next nearest one, it is in order to serve me better. I work hard to see eye to eye with our politicians when they explain that fewer social progams makes for a stronger society. Politics is one subject about which I never seem to think the same as others. I have yet to vote for a candidate who has won a majority. I shouldn't admit this. Politicians will be clamouring for my lack of support.

Differences of opinion are a good thing — except, possibly, at stop signs. I passionately defend other people's right to voice their own opinions. Right up to the point where they disagree with mine.

Perhaps the only thing that all people agree on is that all people will never agree. I sometimes think that if God truly intended us to live together, He wouldn't have given us opinions. But I remind myself that many voices can make one beautiful song. Sometimes differences of opinion baffle me, often they frustrate me and sometimes, as with the gentleman on the Island, they open my eyes to a new and remarkable way of seeing the world. But always, listening to the beliefs someone else holds dear does more than explain how others see their world. It helps me understand my own.

May

Finally spring; the world wakes up each morning now, stretching in warm sunshine. I can almost hear the leaves and crocuses bursting into being along our city streets as the dog and I walk Becky to school on these brilliant, cloudless mornings. All around us, life is beginning again as my children's school year slowly winds to a close. Becky is finishing Grade 6 this year; next fall she'll be off to junior high. These days the conversation on our morning walks is entirely on her final school project, one that has engaged her interest like nothing since she started school at the age of four: choosing an outfit for the Grade 6 graduation dance.

The whole Grade 6 graduation thing is very different now from when I was growing up. In those days, we marked the end of elementary school by getting to go to high school. For my Grade 8 graduation, we had a small assembly in the school gym for which my mother sewed me a fuchsia plaid hot-pants outfit. I thought it was lovely.

In the playground at Becky's school, soccer balls now lie neglected on the field. Knees and elbows are not rough and scraped as usual. The girls who played "Tomb Raider" through the monkey bars in March and brought stuffed animals to slumber parties are now busily plotting wardrobes and hairdos that would stagger a *Vogue* model. Grade 6 Graduation at Allenby Public School requires only slightly less planning and attention than a coronation.

Personally, I think a graduation dance is an excellent way for kids to enter young adulthood. In one trip to the mall to consider dresses and hairstyles, Becky learned several useful life lessons. Lessons such as "99 percent of the population of the world do not buy a $300 dress that they're going to wear for six hours" and "You belong to that 99 percent." I assure Becky that when she grows up and marries either that nice Andrew Leonard she sat beside in Grade 2 or Italian royalty, I will consider buying her a $300 dress. Otherwise, she can do what I did: borrow her mother's.

Some of the hard life-lessons, though, I am sorry my daughter has to face at such a tender age. These would include, "Honey, no amount of hairspray is going to make your hair curl."

For Becky, deciding on the perfect ensemble is still fun. For some mothers I know, the combination of preteen hormones and a major social event is a little like tiptoeing through the mall holding a live grenade. I can't count the number of mothers I saw picking their way through the metaphorical land mines, gingerly trying to steer their daughters away from unsuitable graduation dresses without having the whole situation blow up in their faces. Frankly, these women should not be spending their afternoon negotiating suitable necklines with 12- and 13-year-old girls; they should be out sharing their expertise with career diplomats.

In spite of the pre-event stress, I continue to think that a graduation celebration is an important rite of passage. It's a way of recognizing that our young people are becoming adults. Because sometimes, there is no other way to tell.

My son, Matt, for instance, may be a young man at 15 but so far his greatest claim to adulthood is that I now have to look up at him when I lecture him to turn off the Nintendo. A friend with a son of the same age remarks gloomily that her kid who will be old enough to drive next year can't remember where he left his skateboard last week.

Helping your children become adults is one of the toughest tasks a parent has to face. It means getting them to accept that adulthood means being rational and responsible and this can be hard because, frankly, it means accepting it myself.

As a service to readers with teenagers or pre-teenagers or who just never figured this stuff out for themselves either, I wish to offer three general principles on how to bridge that gap into adulthood.

1. "Adults are responsible."

One of the most common ways to teach your kids responsibility is to get them a pet. Part of our thinking when we got Sparky was that it would help Becky learn about responsibility, and she did. Mostly she learned that she doesn't like it. Matt chose a chinchilla for his pet, which he named Caesar. Many people shy away from chinchillas as pets because of their reputation for being prepared to eat anything. This is totally untrue. It won't eat its chinchilla food. Books, the coffee table and my jacket, however, are fair game. I have told Matt that it's up to him to keep his rodent away from the dog or I will not be responsible for what happens. The chinchilla beats the tar out of the dog.

Another common means of teaching your children responsibility is to assign them chores. I regularly assign tasks to both Matt and Becky. That's because they never actually get around to doing them.

Loosely defined, a chore is any task you could do better yourself, in half the time and with no argument. Chores should always be given with a view to considering time constraints. For example:

Cleaning Becky's room myself = two hours

Getting after Becky to clean her room = six days and four hours

In our house, part of the time is spent just learning each other's languages. For instance, to me a bubble- gum wrapper is garbage. To Becky, it's part of her prized collection of small bits of paper that have accumulated under her bed.

Matt's room is no better. A couple of years ago he fulfilled every teenager's dream and got to relocate his bedroom to the basement. He now refers to Becky and me as "the surface dwellers."

I told myself, when Matt took over the basement, that I could just shut the door and never look at his mess. I can't do it. It's like hiding chocolate in the back of the cupboard — it doesn't matter if you can't see it, you still know it's there. When I venture down to Matt's room, I try hard to convince myself that even Albert Schweitzer likely didn't understand the term "hygiene" when he was 15, that Desmond Tutu probably tossed empty juice cartons under the couch, or that Gandhi left something on his bedroom floor that used to be a banana peel and is now just a gluey, decaying memory of a banana peel. Still, it's all a little discouraging.

The classic means to teach children to be responsible is to let them make their own mistakes. Someone said, "Teach children not to make mistakes by letting them make them." Whoever said this clearly did not value their Teflon pans. So far, Matt and Becky's learning curve has cost me several cooking pots, a living-room carpet and more than a few sleepless nights. I will admit, however, that one of the most memorable lessons of my own teenage years came as a result of accidentally setting fire to my parents' dining-room table. I don't think I'll ever forget that incident, mostly because my siblings now refer to the leaves that you put in tables as kindling.

2. "Adults have values."

I have often said that I want my children to have opinions:

mine. The danger of teaching your children to become the kind of adults who can think for themselves is that, at some point, they will start doing it. I have to admit, I regularly catch myself saying, "Be yourself . . . only not like that."

There comes a time, when a young person stops relying on their parents to teach them values and starts relying on their friends. This is not always a bad thing. Not so long ago, for instance, Becky informed me that she and her friends are "totally off" Britney Spears because she's "just too slutty." I wasn't sure whether to be thrilled or appalled. I think I managed both.

I certainly talk to my children about the values I hold. When we go to movies or watch television, I point out the things I feel are sexist or racist or homophobic or otherwise oppressive. I figure when I've managed to kill their enjoyment of popular culture altogether, my work will be done.

3. "Adults plan for the future."

Just yesterday I was lecturing Matt on the importance of getting things done on time as I was heading out to take down the last of the Christmas lights.

I recall Matt's sixth grade teacher going to great pains at our parent information night to stress the importance of teaching our children to plan ahead. "What we want," she explained, "is for them to become the kind of students in university who do their work in advance and don't just leave it all to the night before it's due." One of the parents raised his hand and asked, "Miss, did you know any students in university like that?" She didn't. Still, it doesn't hurt to dream.

Talking to your children about responsibility with school-work is an excellent way to instill in them an understanding of the future. Keep in mind that when you discuss planning for the future, you mean will they have the grades to get into the college of their choice and they mean will they spend the afternoon playing Nintendo. Encourage them to make a few simple choices now that will help them in the future — like passing.

When it finally is time to talk about university or college, make sure to ask the important questions well in advance. Such as, are you responsible enough to handle the demands of postsecondary education? Do you have a plan for how to use your education in the future? And, will you be taking your pet with you?

I have to say that after all our talks, Matt does now have an idea of what his future could hold. He's going to live with me and become a chinchilla breeder. All I can say is that planning ahead has never seemed more important; I have to get out of here.

Back at the mall, Becky and I head into dress shop NO. 427. She hasn't found the perfect outfit yet. I decide to instill in her the very adult message that "life is compromise" while, at the same time, hoping that it never will be for her.

What techniques can a parent employ to ensure that their children learn to be grownups? Frankly, I haven't a clue. I do know that when all's said and done, there's truth in the saying that "life is the best classroom" — it's one where I'm still learning myself.

Still, my duty as a parent is to at least try to make sure they become caring, responsible people. So, when Matt neglects his homework until Monday morning again or Becky finally hits on the perfect dress, which to my mind is just a little too skimpy and a little too red, it's up to me to do the hardest thing for a parent to do: stand back and watch my children grow up.

Mother's Nature

This morning I announced to my husband, Michael, that I was planning to spend the afternoon romping naked through a spring meadow. He thought I was nuts. "Where are you going to find a babysitter for this afternoon?" He had a point. But as Mother's Day approaches, I've been taking a serious look at my life and I've come to the conclusion that I'm not having enough fun.

Ordinarily I don't feel a need to get back to nature. My kids bring it into the house. Anytime I want to feel earth under my feet, I just take my shoes off in the kitchen. And, I've start composting. So far it's just a pile of laundry in the basement that I've been ignoring for six months, but I'm pretty sure it's started to decompose.

I believe it's important to spend time in the great outdoors. The two weeks our kids spend at camp each summer is an oasis of rest and rejuvenation — for Michael and me, that is. The kids hate it.

It's not communing with nature, though, that makes me want to frolic through a meadow. I simply want to do something unplanned and foolhardy. That makes my family nervous; they think it means I want to redecorate again. Michael suggests that I go to a spa, but I'm not a spa person. I couldn't relax while paying someone $80 an hour to exfoliate my feet. And I don't want to go with out with "the girls" to a male strip show. I can't see paying money to watch some guy throw his clothes on the floor. I can get that at home for free.

What I want is to reconnect with my wild pagan roots. OK, I don't actually have wild pagan roots. I have suburban Baptist roots. While the church provides many wonderful role models, none of them ever had much fun. I remember our Sunday School teacher saying we were not put here to enjoy ourselves. We could honestly assure her that we weren't.

There's no denying that the world is a serious place, particularly when you have children. I have many, many children: two. The financial responsibilities alone are enormous. When your children are in diapers, you have to start planning for their future after high school. Our current plan is hoping they'll run away and join the circus.

In the meantime, my children need expensive luxuries such as food and housing. We're lucky to own our own home. Well, we say we own it. Our bank owns it and lets us live in it. We own one-half of the upstairs closet. Our part is immaculate, but you wouldn't believe the mess the bank's part is in.

Preparing for the future is a good thing. Frankly, whoever said you should "live in the moment" never car-pooled. Somehow, though, the serious things in life seem to happen whether you're ready for them or not.

I remember when Matt was a baby. My daily routine was to get up in the morning, get Matt up, feed Matt, dress Matt, dress myself, get Matt's stuff packed up, get Matt in the car, drive Matt to daycare, unpack Matt, unpack Matt's stuff. One morning I got back into the car, and two thoughts occurred to me. First, when Orders of Canada are handed out they should go to the women who get their children to daycare on the bus. Second, here I was limp, exhausted, having put in a full day's work and I hadn't even been to the office yet. I loved my child, I loved my life, but somehow it wasn't a lot of fun.

Mother's Day is an excellent time to think seriously about our roles as mothers. This year I choose as my role model Mother Nature: nurturing, sustaining, also wonderful and wild. I may not romp naked through a meadow. Naked is a relative term anyway as I've reminded Michael on cold winter nights when he wants to be romantic. What I am planning to do is give the seriousness of life a little kick in the grass, maybe dance barefoot in the backyard. It's a frivolous, senseless, foolish thing to do. And I've earned it.

Who You Gonna Call?

This morning I'm going out to return a shirt I bought for my daughter, Becky. It's a lovely shirt. Turquoise stretch knit with a bubble-gum-pink feathered collar, this shirt is the final word in elementary school chic. Becky loves its style. She loves the colour. It fits perfectly and it's exactly like the ones her friends Saxon and Sheena are wearing. There is only one thing wrong with this shirt. I picked it out.

Don't get me wrong; I'm happy that Becky wants to choose her own clothes. I like my children to have an opinion. That's why I'm always trying to give them mine. But as I head out to return Becky's shirt, drop off the trumpet she called in a panic to say she'd forgotten and the lunch bag my son Matt hasn't yet realized he's forgotten, I can't help but marvel at how soon children stop needing a parent.

"Give your children independence, not advice." At least that's what my mother is always telling me. But, with Mother's Day approaching, I'm starting to wonder what my role as a parent really is.

This shouldn't surprise me. I realized years ago that the most important role of my life is one where the job description seems to change daily. Just yesterday, for instance, my role was to watch my children's every move, steer them away from inappropriate behaviour and keep them safe. Now that they're teenagers . . . actually that part hasn't changed very much.

I don't mind Matt and Becky becoming more independent. I just think we should do it together. I can't even remember when my children's move toward independence began. Probably the day they were born. At the age of 10 months Matt decided it was time to feed himself. He could hold a spoon. He could pick up spaghetti. The fact that he couldn't actually hit his mouth didn't faze him for an instant. For most of her early school years, Becky would only answer to the name "Iguana." I supported Becky in her creative thinking but it was not a bright moment in my life when I sat in the school auditorium and heard the award for Best Sharing in the Sandbox go to "Iguana Hines." The fact that the woman sitting three seats away had actually named her daughter Skylark did not comfort me for a moment.

As my children have gotten older, their choices have become more daunting. Letting them choose their own clothes I can deal with. I realize that, at a certain age, children need to challenge the norm and express their individuality. They seem to do this by all dressing and acting alike. The day Becky started sporting her "personal style" was the day I could no longer pick her out in the schoolyard.

Other choices I find more challenging. Becky wants a career that showcases her intellect and integrity, just like P!NK. Matt grew his hair shoulder length, which I learned to accept — then he dyed it green. My current strategy when they share their latest scheme is simply to smile supportively and chant to myself, "It's not drugs. It's not drugs."

I remind myself that at any age children need things only a mother can provide. Food and clean laundry seem to be the two most important ones. But my children have moved in the blink of an eye from fretting and complaining if I wasn't around to fretting and complaining if I am.

There's no reason to be confused about my role as a mother. Lots of people are prepared to explain it to me. No job in the world provides so little training and so much scrutiny. In fact, I love the job of being a parent; it's the performance reviews that are killing me. I recall trips to the grocery store where, within two aisles, one fellow shopper advised me that my children should be wearing sweaters and another observed that their hats must be making them too warm.

My local bookstore is crammed with counsel on exactly what it takes to be a good parent. I've never bought the idea that the people who write these things are parents, just like me. For one thing, they have time to write all those books. According to these experts, in order to prepare for life after the children no longer need me, I have to do more than simply hold down a job and look after my family; I need to set personal goals. I do that. Usually my goal is "Try to make it through the day." I suppose I could be more ambitious. Maybe something along the lines of "Try to make it though the day sane."

I should probably talk to my own mother about the changes I'm experiencing. My mother and I have a pretty traditional mother/daughter relationship. I just want her to love me. And be available whenever I need her. Oh, and help me out with things from time to time. And listen to my constant whining. Also, I want to be treated like an adult. When it comes to my current dilemma, though, I don't think Mom could help. She's an intelligent empathetic person, but a woman of her generation has no idea of the emotional and physical toll involved in trying to maintain a full-time job and caring for Matt and Becky. All my mother had to do was stay home all day and take care of five children.

I did try calling Mom once to ask how she deals with the trauma and confusion of her children no longer needing her. She was out. A woman's place may be in the home but these days, as far as my mother's concerned, only if it's someone else's home and there's a bridge game involved.

Well into her sixties, my mother went back to school and became a minister. She taught English in Prague. In summer, she plays tennis; in winter, she skis. The year she turned 70, Mom said she was taking a trip by herself to South America "before I get old." A family friend prudently arranged for her to have a local guide. Excellent idea — my brothers and sisters and I could keep tabs on Mom's movements. We did hear from the guide often. He would call every morning screaming, "Mrs. Sim! I cannot find Mrs. Sim!" Apparently, if the man wasn't in the lobby by 6 a.m., my mother just left without him.

I'm grateful that my mother is self-sufficient, but I keep waiting for signs that she's starting to need me more. Sure enough, a week ago she called, anxious and concerned, "Anne, someone stole my vacuum cleaner." I was gentle: "Mom, you're nuts."

"No, really, I had a blue vacuum cleaner and now . . . oh wait . . . this is mine." It had been so long since she'd vacuumed, she'd forgotten what it looked like. In the end, we both decided this was a good thing.

What I've learned from my mother is that independence is a state of mind. I mind that my children are independent. But the reality of being a parent is that I have to let my children go. Over and over again. And perhaps the best way to help them learn to enjoy their independence is to start enjoying my own.

So, this Mother's Day, I will spend the day with my children savouring the glorious feeling of being needed . . . and the evening with my mother savouring the glorious feeling of not being needed all the time. The day will come when laundry, meals, the choice of what clothes they will wear or what lives they will lead will be entirely up to my children. But when will they stop needing my love and support? My mother smiles with the wisdom of a mother who has lived these changes, "I'm still waiting."

Summer

June

Warm afternoons, soft evenings that seem long enough to stretch into September.

Like March, the month of June is named for an ancient deity, the goddess Juno, patroness of midsummer, the prime of the year and protector of women and marriage. I was married in June, leading me to think that perhaps the goddess and I have a few things to discuss. In fact, I have many happy memories of my years of being married. What I try to remember most often is that the hallmark of a good relationship is not necessarily that it lasts forever.

June is the season of fruition. My daughter was born in June, a gift from the goddess if ever there was one. Ina, the raconteur of our dog park, says that in Baltic countries, wild strawberries ripen in June and people feast on them as a delicacy. My friends Cheryl and Avi each celebrate Shavuot around this time, a Jewish festival of the first harvest. In olden days, the Saxons danced naked in the forests on Midsummer's Eve, a magical time of fruition and fulfillment celebrated with wine, song and debauchery. I have every intention of honouring this tradition by dancing fully clothed in the living room and having a non-diet Coke. Debauchery is kind of a relative term.

The summer solstice on June 21 is the middle age of the year, a time when the sun is at its most glorious, most radiant, most powerful, even as it begins to wane just a little. Somehow, I relate to this. Of course, I'm nowhere near being middle-aged myself . . . providing I live to be 120.

I have to admit, though, that small signs of middle age may be creeping in. Shopping at the mall with my girlfriend Liz last week, I spotted the most astonishing pair of summer sandals. Sturdy, no-nonsense sandals, with pretty much the same weight and fashion flare as two concrete blocks. I loved them. Incredibly, they were also on sale. Liz said they were "old lady shoes." They were not old lady shoes. I bet her we could walk through the entire mall and not see one elderly woman wearing sandals like that. And we didn't. We saw an elderly man.

I'm not ready to see myself as middle-aged yet. Some ancient poet said, "Age is to women like the ripeness of fine fruit." Personally, I can't quite convince myself that it's romantic that I'm becoming squishy. Of course, that poet had something that kept him from seeing how alarming middle age can be: he was a man.

To be fair, men may have just as hard a time as women coping with the onset of middle age. After all, more men than women seem to have midlife crises. There's a reason for this. We don't have time. Besides, a man may wake up one morning, look in the mirror and say, "Oh my gosh! I can't believe my hair! And I look so drawn and haggard! And I had no idea life was going to be like this!" Most women I know have been doing that since we were in our twenties.

I think, the truth is, anyone can be pulled up short by middle age. It happens the day you realize that instead of asking, "What am I going to do today?" you're somehow asking, "What am I going to do with my life?" The difference seems to be that when a man suddenly needs to find himself, he goes out and finds a sports car or a younger spouse. A woman who wants to find herself almost always ends up in tight exercise clothes or difficult university courses.

A few things occurred in my own life around early middle age that made me stop and ask, "Who am I?" Previous to this, I had mostly only asked, "Where am I?" I have a habit of coming out of buildings or off buses and walking with supreme confidence in the wrong direction. Figuring out where I was going in my life was shaping up to be even tougher. I knew who I was in relationship with other people, of course; I was Michael's wife, Matt and Becky's mom, Bruce, Keltie, David and Kathryn's sister, Otha's daughter, Cheryl's friend; I just didn't have a clue who I was in relationship to myself. A friend of mine says, "Life is a journey. I want to know something about the person I'm travelling with." I needed to "find myself." As I've said before, this was a fairly radical concept for a woman who normally has trouble finding her car keys.

One of the things that happened was my marriage ended. I have to admit, I saw it coming. You know you're in trouble the day you realize you've put your couples counsellor on speed dial.

Life trials such as divorce can be catalysts to finding yourself. It is certainly a catalyst to finding a lawyer. Michael and I had a team of experts working on our case: two lawyers, a couples counsellor, a mediator, two accountants. These people are trained to help you divide your assets amicably — mostly, it seems, by ensuring that you don't have anything left to fight about when you've paid their bills.

I learned a lot from this process. For instance, the best way to look at a divorce agreement is to consider it a peace treaty. Depending on what issue's on the table, one of you gets to be the government and the other is a First Nations band. Be prepared for the moments when "living off the land" seems like your only hope for survival. Like most couples who have been married for some time, Michael and I had spent years accumulating the usual stuff of married life — debt. But, there is something you do not divide. Love for our children, Michael and I will always share equally.

Divorce wasn't the only life change that spurred me to think about my life.

Some years before, I had quit my full-time job, which was overwhelmingly demanding, to stay home with my young children — which turned out to be more overwhelmingly demanding. There were upsides to quitting work outside the home. I was no longer troubled at dinner parties by anyone asking my opinion about anything, and the problem of "where to have lunch" was pretty much answered by "Beef-a-Roni at home with the kids." I have to admit though, after the first four or five months, the glow started to wear off.

I began to set my alarm for 4:30 a.m. every morning, get up and go downstairs and write a novel. Looking back, this seems like kind of a strange thing to do — I mean, who writes a novel? I used to call the time I got up 30 minutes to 5 because anyone who would get up at 4:30 a.m. to do anything was just weird. I don't for a moment think that I'm particularly disciplined. If someone asked me to get up at 4:30 a.m. to go jogging, I couldn't have done it. I did this because I needed a few hours to be myself before I spent the rest of the day being everything else.

Writing a book was a kind of therapy. I also started to look for wisdom about who I was in the only place it can be found: everywhere.

I took yoga classes. My yoga instructor was a deeply spiritual person who believed that people are brought into your life for a purpose. Mine, apparently, was to make her regret not having become a dental hygienist instead. She encouraged us to find a mantra to use in the meditation portion of our classes, some meaningful message we needed to convey to ourselves. Apparently, "Remember to pick up milk" was just not zen enough for her. She also explained that meditation is the art of learning to still the mind, to stretch out the time between your rational thoughts. I figured I'd be great at this because I hadn't had a rational thought in months. With a lot of careful instruction and patience, I did get better at being able to leave my worries outside of the room during our sessions. To my mind, though, real success would have been being able to tiptoe by my worries without them noticing me on the way out.

I went to a "self-imaging" workshop, which I also failed miserably. When our facilitator challenged us to consider, "Who do you truly want to be?" all I could think was "Michelle Pfeiffer!"

I read many, many books. Most of the writers offered the same unwavering guidance: "Think for yourself." One book suggested I work to overcome the desire for material possessions by purchasing their accompanying "journal and workbook" for $24.99. All I can say is that anyone who says money can't buy happiness has never been to a really great shoe sale.

It wouldn't be fair to say that none of these people or books helped in my search for myself. They did finally lead me to ask myself some really hard questions such as, "What do I want?" Hard, because most of my experience had been asking, "What do other people need?" This is more than a subtle shift in thought.

In the book that I wrote, the heroine goes alone one June to Cape Breton Island. She doesn't know where she is and she doesn't know that she's capable of looking after herself.

She also doesn't know that what she really needs to find is, not her location on this island, but her place in her own life. I went alone into not being a wife, not being a worker, not knowing what I wanted beyond what I'd been told I should have. One thing I learned is that trying to find yourself is a very lonely, very scary, very challenging journey and I wouldn't have missed it for the world. I now know that the only mistakes are experiences I didn't learn from and that, even if I don't always recognize the road ahead of me that doesn't mean for a moment that I'm going in the wrong direction.

The summer solstice is the moment in the journey of the sun when it is at its most powerful. I am at that time in my own life. Young enough to embrace this journey. Old enough to know something now about the person I'm taking it with. Young enough to pursue my dreams. Old enough to know what they might be. Young enough to believe in love. Old enough to know what that looks like for me. I, like the year, am in the prime of my life. I am at my most radiant, my most splendid, my most powerful. And how long will this feeling of being glorious in my own life last? I think until I'm 120.

House Rules

At the time my second child was born, I was holding down a full-time job where the people were demanding, the expectations huge and the hours endless. Then I would leave home and go to the office.

When I became a mother, colleagues assumed that I would prefer to stay home. I joked, "Are you kidding? There are children there!" But between office and family I wasn't finding time for the little things like eating, breathing or using the bathroom.

I'm not sure why I thought quitting my job to stay home would make life simpler. Perhaps a woman with small children, a husband, pets and a full-time job is not capable of making clear-headed decisions. If she were, she wouldn't have all those things. My friends said if I quit work I'd be crazy in six months. They were wrong. It only took three.

A day at home with the kids was twice as hard as a day at the office. I always valued my co-workers for the important things they gave me — their scissors and staplers — but now the longest conversation I had with an adult was when I thanked the grocery store cashier for my change. When asked what it was like to quit work, I looked at the laundry, the grocery list and the kids' mess and said, "I have no idea."

Becky started nursery school and suddenly I had time alone. Two hours a day. I didn't know whether to take up neurosurgery or write a novel. I decided to try working from home — it would stimulate my brain and give me personal satisfaction. Also, we thought it would be nice to be able to afford food again.

For those considering leaving their jobs, lunches, colleagues and real clothes to work from home, I have some helpful words: "What, are you crazy?" Having said that, here's the "HineSight Guide to Home-Office Work."

1. Best thing about working from home: The commute.

2. Dress code: If you're wearing clothes, you're dressed well enough. Overdressed is wearing clothes you didn't sleep in. Someday, fashion houses will recognize the untapped market and produce specialty clothes for home-office workers — designer ratty bathrobes.

3. Technology: Internet access is key to saving time. Without it you will waste hours thinking up your own ways to avoid work. You will need e-mail, a sophisticated message system developed by the most brilliant minds of our time. It allows me to instantly contact my friend Marni in Vancouver with vital information such as "The dog threw up on the carpet again." You will also want to be able to chat online in real time with home-office workers around the world so you can exchange ideas, information, support and Space Invaders strategies.

4. Support groups: Get to know the people who can help you in your work. For instance, my local coffee-shop clerk cuts me off after the third latte. These guys are modern-day heroes. They spend their whole day dealing with customers who haven't had coffee yet. I could drink decaf, but drinking decaf is like having sex with your clothes on. Sure, you can do it, but why would you?

5. Discipline: It's said that the key to working from home is concentration, but I never pay any attention to that.

Teach your family to respect your privacy. The best way to do that is to say "Let me read you what I'm working on!" every time they come near.

Working from home has made me very sociable. Telemarketers hang up on me because they have work to do.

Occasionally, inspiration hits. Inspiration is a resplendent once-in-a-lifetime idea that occurs at 2 a.m. when there are no pens around for 800 miles. "Oh yes! This idea will write itself!" I say. The next morning I fire up the computer, and it hasn't.

Working from home hasn't made life any less hectic or challenging, but it has taught me something about the perfect way to balance work and family life. There isn't one.

Food Rights

My son, Matt, has been diagnosed with allergies. It's pretty straightforward: he just can't eat food.

It isn't the first time in my life that food has caused me problems. The two most memorable fights of my marriage were about food. In our first week as a married couple, we argued over how much milk goes into scrambled eggs. Looking back now I can see that this was a childish, petty disagreement that could have been avoided entirely if Michael had just admitted that you do not put a single teaspoon of milk in with four eggs. Our second fight was over quiche. Michael said that if I took quiche to a potluck supper, his friends would think I was showing off. That was before he'd seen my quiche.

Feeding our children has always been tricky. At 18 months Matt enjoyed food largely for its recreational value: he fingerpainted with it, played catch with it, did anything but actually put it in his mouth. A friend, whose son is now six foot four, assured me that from ages 2 to 11, he ate nothing but crackers with mayonnaise.

For years my house seemed covered in a thin glaze of apple juice. You could eat off my kitchen floor — that's where most of the food ended up. I devised a foolproof way for using up the kids' leftovers: I ate them. A diet guru suggested spraying glass cleaner on leftovers to eliminate temptation. It's a good idea. Glass cleaner on grilled cheese tastes terrible. Not that I know that.

As my children got older, food suddenly became interesting: it came with a toy. We ate fast-food burgers, which had the daily caloric allowance for a small country. Our meals at home were much better. If the four food groups were fat, sugar, salt and pyridoxine hydrochloride, we were eating a wonderfully balanced diet.

Now I read ingredient lists. I have advice about reading labels: Don't do it! The list of preservatives in many products is as long as my arm. No wonder people are living longer. My new rule is "Don't buy anything with more than two ingredients you can't pronounce."

Finding food Matt can eat means shopping at health food stores. My first trip was overwhelming. I recall standing in the organic-meat section, trying to figure out the difference between free-range and organically fed. I burst into tears. A clerk sympathized, "I know, ma'am. I don't think we should sell meat either."

I've learned a few things about health food. When farmers don't have to pay for pricey pesticides and antibiotics, their food somehow becomes much more expensive. Also, all health food has one thing in common: it's brown.

I am grateful that I can afford the food that Matt needs. But eating gluten-free, sugar-free and, I must admit, sometimes taste-free has been tough on him. At 15 years of age he's not much into sports, and romance is still a distant, hazy dream. Food has been a dependable pleasure. Somehow I can relate.

Matt's situation makes me think of a revolt against oppressive working conditions that took place in the United States in 1912. Actually, many things in my life make me think of a revolt against oppressive working conditions. In this case women textile workers rallied around a demand for Bread and Roses. Besides a fair wage, they wanted respect and beauty in their lives.

Learning to eat healthily has made me a crusader — for chocolate cupcakes. The next time I donate tuna and peanut butter to our local food bank, I'll add chocolate bars and quality coffee. It's the flavour of life, the little pleasures I give myself and others, that makes it worthwhile.

Maybe, in time, I'll find a way to make Matt's favourite cookie-dough ice cream out of carrot shavings. Until then I'll splurge guiltlessly now and then and buy him a really great mango. Bread, I am blessed to have; now I'm going outside to smell the roses.

July

Summer settles on the city like a damp dish-towel. Too hot to garden. Too hot to cook. Too hot to work in my tiny, un-air-conditioned workroom. As far as I'm concerned, this weather could last forever.

By the beginning of July, I have already applied about 183 layers of sunscreen. I am a great believer in responsible exposure to the sun. Often, I end the season whiter than when I started out.

A strange feeling always comes over me at this point in the summer. I want to buy fashion magazines. There I am, standing in my local convenience store, just about to reach for my copy of *Home Workers Monthly: The Bathrobe Issue*, when suddenly, I want to buy *Vogue*. I want to buy *marie claire*; I want to buy anything with Claudia Shiffer on the cover.

In any other month, reading a feature like "A Better Butt In 30 Days" would have about much appeal to me as checking the ingredient list on a box of Twinkies. I'm not drawn in by touching articles on how money can't buy happiness, sandwiched between two 10-page spreads of outfits starting at $500 that assure us that it absolutely does. And when Vera Wang starts designing "Fall fashions to wear on the school trip to the bug farm," we'll talk. But somehow, July rolls around and suddenly I'm blowing my iced coffee budget on *Glamour* and *Bazaar*.

I think, the truth is, that reading these magazines reminds me of simpler times. Not better, but simpler. They remind me of a time when I had a summer job and a disposable income. When clean towels magically reproduced themselves in the bathroom cupboard and life could be sustained on french fries and gravy alone. To me, these magazines are not just insubstantial flights of fashion fancy; they're an essential life tool. Particularly on hazy summer days when it's too hot to waste time in all the usual ways. Over the years, fashion magazines have become one of my summer traditions.

I have to say, I've always been a big believer in tradition. My daughter, Becky, recently got asked out on her first "date." "Jordan" dealt with the usual incapacitating terror of rejection by bypassing the tradition of speaking to Becky in person and, instead sent an e-mail that went something like this, "My dad says you can come to the basketball game with us if you want." Seeing this, frankly, I was annoyed. Why didn't they have e-mail when I was her age?

Near the end of the month, Becky, Matt, and I pack up the car and follow our summer tradition of going to the cottage. Our family cottage is the ultimate in idyllic situations; my mother owns it, my mother maintains it and we all get to use it every summer.

Cottaging comes with its own traditions. One of the most entrenched is to look down on anyone with a more palatial spread than you as "not real cottagers." In cottage terms, "basic is beautiful." A spacious deck, wall-to-wall broadloom or an efficient plumbing system can all push you into the "not real cottagers" category, in the eyes of someone who's living a little closer to the land than you. This has always been a difficult standard for my family to live down to. My mother's idea of "roughing it in the bush" is that the microwave only has three settings. The year she threatened to redo the living room in chintz, we knew we'd be limited to looking down our noses at people who had two-car garages or satellite dishes.

The biggest claim to "backwoods chic" at our family cottage is that we have never had a television. My parents' reasoning was, "We want you spending your time out of doors, romping in the meadows, splashing in the lake or maybe, if it's raining, reading or playing board games." We understood entirely. They didn't want us to have any fun.

Now that I'm a parent, it's my turn to listen to children whining, "Why can't we have a TV here?" I explain to Matt and Becky that it's the same reason I made them take piano lessons or drink all their milk: because my parents did it to me.

It's Matt who complains most these days, particularly since he's hit his teenage years. One of the biggest changes brought on by puberty is that chasing minnows in the river or building fortresses out of sticks and old sheets are no longer the absorbing day-long activities they used to be. One summer evening, I met him coming up from the beach in the twilight. "I watched the sunset," he said. "It was the only thing on." The next night, I joined him for the rerun.

Family cottages, much like Christmas, are all about tradition. Which is not surprising, because families are all about tradition. It's nice to know that however much the world seems to change, your relationship with your family always stays the same. At least you know what you're up against.

Loosely defined, tradition is anything you do a certain way because that's how you've always done it. In the case of some traditions, it's still possible to trace the reason for why they exist. Take, for instance, the tradition of really ugly bridesmaids' dresses. There is a reason why brides dress their closest friends in the entire world in outfits that make them look like walking cabbages; it's because they can.

For other traditions, though, the origins have somehow been lost in the mists of time. Like wearing skirts. Why do we wear skirts? It's not for practical reasons. No 18th-century pioneer woman was ever heard to utter the words, "Fighting off wolves and leaning over an open fire all day is just so much easier in a skirt." No woman today says, "I'd just love to work from home because I could spend all day in a skirt," or "I'm trekking up the 'hell' side of Kilimanjaro next month. I think I'll wear a skirt," or "I'm so glad I have a skirt because, otherwise, I'd have no reason to buy pantyhose." Other baffling traditions are why we call Easter "Easter,"* or why we use an Italian name to order large-size drinks in coffee shops that originated in the western United States.

The traditions of our family cottage are no more explicable. An example of this is our system for disposing of garbage, which goes something like this: all food waste goes into a small plastic grocery bag, slung over the door handle in the kitchen. Sometimes the bag tips, which is not good. Sometimes it falls off. Often we run out of bags and have to talk someone into doing a milk run before we can continue cleaning up. When you want to go out the door where the bag is hanging, you have to shove it out of your way. When the bag is full (which, in a household of 20-some people happens about every 16 seconds), it's removed and put into a large garbage bag in the furnace room where the challenge is to get it to the local dump before it starts to smell or the dog becomes curious about it. When my friend Liz visited one summer, she suggested that instead of using the small bags, we put the garbage

---

*For those of you who won't sleep tonight now that I've brought this up, I took the time to find out. It was making me nuts too. As Christianity spread through the region that is now Germany in about the 7th century, the church elders of the day felt that the easiest way to integrate Christian observance into a pagan culture would be to hold the new feast days at the same times as the old. The celebration to mark Jesus' resurrection was named "Easter" when it replaced the pagan spring festival of "Eostara," goddess of fertility and rebirth. Who knew, eh?

directly into the large bags, placed in actual covered bins. A breathtaking innovation. Of course, we didn't do it. It wasn't tradition.

Every afternoon in the summer we go in the boat to the little town of Dorset for frozen yogurt. Every evening we sit down to play cards and my brother Bruce gets huffy and vows he will never play euchre with any family member again. On every family weekend, there is one argument about politics. Someone gets upset because another sibling's kids are making noise in the lake while their kids are napping. We take turns complaining that we are the only one who ever buys toilet paper. My mother sits and thumbs through decorating magazines with articles like "20 Ways to Make Your Cottage Indistinguishable From a City Condo." Over the years, I've found a way to deal with our family quirks; they make me nuts.

But also, I love them. Family traditions are like families themselves: sometimes irrational, often repetitive, and almost always as predictable as the waves on our beach. This year, everything at the cottage will be exactly the same as it has been every other year. In other words, it will be just right.

On any sunny afternoon, as I head down to the hammock with this year's pile of fashion magazines, I'll hear Bruce up at the cottage, asking who's up for cards tonight. My sister Keltie will be off to the store because we're out of small plastic bags. It will remind me again that some things don't change.

But some things do. What has changed over the years is that the things that matter to me now are not what's in the magazines I tote to the beach each July — the lure of thinner thighs or my chances of starting the fall with a Donna Karan wardrobe. They're a healthy family, challenging work and times just like these with the people I love. My dreams today might not be as glamorous as the ones encouraged by these glossy magazines, but they're more precious than a Chanel suit and more enduring than the perfect summer tan.

Mind over Manners

If there's one thing that makes me want to spit, it's people who don't know how to behave properly. I was thinking that this morning as I was standing in my local grocery store, taste-testing the bulk olives. A woman with a full cart of groceries was waiting in the checkout line, completely ignoring the person behind her who had only a head of lettuce. Where I come from, that is just bad manners. You don't stand with your 50 items in front of someone who has only one or two. Not without making a show of looking at your watch every five seconds and murmuring audibly, "Oh gosh, I'm really trying to look as if I'm in a rush to get to the deathbed of my nearest relative who asked for these groceries as her last request and I know you're not falling for this, but like I care." I mean, it's only polite.

Manners are what separate us from the animals. That and, of course, credit cards. Growing up, my parents always made it clear to my siblings and me that we were to treat other people with kindness and civility and that, if we didn't, we were going to get it. To this day, my mother threatens to contact the parents of telemarketers who disturb her during the dinner hour.

As an adult, I have come to see that there is a right way and a wrong way to do everything. Loosely defined, the right way to do things is how I do them myself. For instance, it is just not civilized behaviour to hover over someone's table in a busy coffee shop, eyeing her half-finished chai tea until she finally lets you have her seat. The well-bred thing to do is stand quietly at a discreet distance until the table is vacated and then elbow anyone out of your way who tries to get there first.

I have to admit that knowing all the finer points of etiquette is not always easy. I recall coming home once from an elegant dinner party with an adorable little dog statue that I'd found placed by my plate as a party favour. A telephone call the next morning asked if I'd please return my hostess's antique knife rest.

Easy or not, etiquette is important. Good manners are not just arbitrary. There's a reason for doing things the way we do them — we just have no idea what it is. I was trying to explain this the other night to my children, who, I'm ashamed to say, have been allowed to develop less-than-perfect manners, especially at the table. Still, I expect Matt and Becky to show a little civility at mealtimes. A lot would be out of the question.

At this particular family dinner, I caught Matt buttering his baked potato with his finger. I immediately pointed out to him that this is not polite behaviour at the table, even though it meant interrupting my cellphone call to tell him off. It occurred to me at that moment, though, that perhaps all of us could use a little brushing up on our manners.

I blame our sorry eating habits on the busy stressful work we live in today. A formal dinner at our house means that we watch the arts channel instead of *The Simpsons* while we eat. But the way I figured it, I had nothing to lose by trying to improve my family's table manners except, possibly, my sanity.

First step: find out how we should be doing things. I went to the library and managed to locate an aged etiquette book. Not very helpful, seeing how there was no mention of what fork to use when eating out of a Styrofoam container. The more I read, though, the more I found it reassuring. The writer of the book was a woman who had taught table etiquette to diplomats and heads of state, which just goes to prove one thing: none of them know how to behave properly either.

This writer cautioned me against the lax practice of substituting teaspoons when I should be using sorbet spoons. I can honestly say I have never done that. She also suggested that if I regularly take my children to the opera, ballet and art galleries, I will never have to worry about their manners. It's true. They'll go live with the neighbours.

The times and manners have changed since this book was written, but I decided that having a formal dinner as a setting for table manner instruction still makes sense. I would show my children that serviettes do not come from a roll on the counter and that "finger food" is not a term synonymous with "anything on your plate." I'll introduce Matt and Becky to elegant food, properly chosen cutlery and cloth napkins. Of course, this would require significant preparatory work on my part. I had to find a restaurant I could afford.

After rooting through the restaurant reviews in the newspaper, I decided to get out the big guns — boot camp for etiquette. We were going to the fanciest French restaurant in town.

The children were immediately responsive. They whined.
"Why do we have to go to a fancy restaurant?"
"Because you have terrible table manners."
"Then shouldn't you leave us at home?"

I broke it to Matt that he would have to put on nice clothes. He was appalled. "What, you mean like . . . clean?" No, I meant a jacket and tie.
"Why do I have to wear a jacket and tie?"
"So you'll feel comfortable."

I could feel my credibility slipping away by the second. Becky groused, "Will they have burgers and fries?"
"No, they'll have nice food. French food."
"Poutine?"

Matt suggested we bring the etiquette book with us in case there was something I didn't know. "We do not read at the table," I said grandly. The lesson had begun.

The restaurant was amazing. Not a plastic tray or all-you-can-eat dessert bar in sight. A distinguished-looking waiter with an elegant French accent presented our menus. Becky, whose idea of a great dining experience is to graze the free-sample aisle at Costco, immediately had questions: "How can they charge this much for food?" I informed her that, when at the table, we do not comment loudly on the price of the meal.

Matt wanted to know how to eat a breadstick: "Do you hold the end or are you supposed to break it into chunks first?" I should have brought the book.

Becky complained audibly that for $14.50 you should get the whole frog, not just the legs. Our waiter returned for our order and Becky piped up, "I'll have the $28 piece of beef." I suggested, with restraint, that this is not a proper way to order.

She tried again, "I'll have the $28 piece of beef, please." Our waiter smiled charmingly, "Would the young lady care to have fries with that?" I didn't care what this was costing me. I loved him.

Matt deftly ordered bisque to start, followed by lobster pâté served over sweet-pea wafers with a compote of seasonal vegetables. "I watch the Food Network, Mom." This was very impressive, especially since I recall, when I was a teenager, sending vichyssoise back to the restaurant kitchen because it was cold.

While we waited for our meal the kids started bickering over the rolls and I outlined the importance of making pleasant dinner conversation. "Let's talk about something we're all interested in." Silence. Matt remembered that he had a new video game involving dead rodents. I suggested we discuss it another time, particularly as I had ordered the rabbit.

Our meal arrived and I launched into my demonstration. "We tear the bread into pieces. We hold our glass by the bowl, not the stem. We do not slurp our water. When Becky snorts water through her nose, we do not laugh, thus encouraging her to do it again, do we?" I was starting to feel like Queen Victoria.

Our waiter was like the perfect lover — entirely present and attentive when I wanted him and off happily engaged somewhere else when I didn't. He conversed cordially with Matt on the subjects of crème caramel preparation and the dead rodent game. He whisked Becky's entrée away to remove the offending Provençal, from the beef Provençal.

Etiquette-wise, we did pretty well. Food did end up in the lap, a dinner knife got used instead of a butter knife and the wrong spoon entirely went into the soup. The kids weren't perfect either. Through it all, our waiter smiled and assisted and made us feel downright correct. It reminded me of what my father used to say about manners, "Real class is making other people feel like they have it." When the time came to pay the very large tip, I did so gratefully. A small price to pay for a good lesson in manners. Mostly, I have to say, for me.

In the end, neither my children nor I came home from our dinner out with the kind of high-toned polish required by that etiquette book. The good news is we have enough social graces to feel comfortable in social situations. And, for my part, I think I remembered what good manners, the best of manners, are all about. Etiquette is not simply knowing what's acceptable. It's about being accepting.

With Thanks

This morning my neighbour Cheryl did a really mean thing. She brought me a coffee. I don't understand it. Ordinarily Cheryl is exactly what you want in a neighbour — compared to us, she has a worse lawn and a better snow shovel. I can't believe Cheryl, of all people, would suddenly do something like bring me a cup of coffee. Now I will have to go out and buy her a car.

There may be truth in the saying "It is more blessed to give than receive," but for me, it's also easier. If I do something for someone else, it's an act of good-spirited, unadulterated kindness. If they do something for me, it's extortion. I know this is a double standard — just like if I leave my Christmas lights up until May it's because I lead a full, busy life, but if my neighbours do it, it's because they just can't get their act together. I don't mind employing double standards for myself but I hate it when other people do it.

I admit that I often equate thoughtfulness with obligation. I've been known to send thank-you notes for thank-you notes. I consider people who practise "random acts of kindness" emotional terrorists. I worry about being under an obligation so great that no gift basket will ever free me. I'm in a cold sweat all through December, agonizing that someone not "on my list" will do something horrendous like give me a present. I know I'll respond by frantically gift wrapping my microwave.

I don't know why I find it so difficult to accept help and attention from others. It's certainly not something I learned from my family. Years ago when my brother Bruce invited the family to dinner at his first apartment, my mother asked if she could bring anything. Bruce replied, "Roast beef, mashed potatoes and something for dessert."

I must say, I don't always find it hard to let people do things for me. There are times when I can very graciously accept help from others — when I'm paying them. Instead of venting to my friends, for instance, I see a therapist. I didn't get this from my family either. My father used to say, "Anyone who would consult a psychiatrist needs to have his head examined." The way I see it, I am not paying my therapist $60 an hour to listen to my problems. I am paying her $60 an hour so I do not have to listen to hers in return. A therapist trains for many years to be qualified to let you work everything out on your own. This must be a great job. My friend, Avi, a psychologist, says it would be perfect except that people are constantly coming to him with their problems.

I have also, on occasion, paid someone to help clean my house. My mother always said that cleanliness is next to godliness. For me, cleanliness is next to impossible. On two occasions I did decide to hire some help because Matt and Becky had started complaining that the soap scum in the shower was talking to them. (I just wish I could train it to say, "Wash behind your ears.") I am not one of those people who hire a cleaning person and then feel they have to tidy up before she arrives. To me, that's ridiculous. I simply didn't let her into any of the rooms I was embarrassed about. This poor woman would sweep the front hall and spend the rest of the day sitting on the stairs with a cup of tea.

I know exactly what my neighbour Cheryl expects in return for this cup of coffee: absolutely nothing. But to my mind, I am now bound to her in eternal gratitude, which, on reflection, I think is a good thing. Because when it comes to accepting something from others, be it coffee or caring, I do have an obligation: to allow my friends the same happiness in giving to me as I get from giving to them.

August

The month of August swelters and swoons through long hazy afternoons, time suddenly content to move at the pace of snails on the shore.

On days like these, the idea of "eternity" seems something conjured up by a vacationer lying in a hammock under a shady pine and not, as I've usually believed, a word developed to describe the time span of a birthday party for seven-year-olds.

Today, it seems possible to believe that the sky will never turn from the turquoise shades of July into the indigo blue of fall. That the crispness that now comes in the morning air is simply a summer storm on the breeze and not the first faint chill of autumn. August is a month that encourages such denial. I lie on the beach during my summer vacation at the cottage and plot a citizen's arrest of retailers who show fall fashions before the end of the month.

It's not only the advent of fall that it seems possible to deny in August. Even day-to-day demands on my time can be pushed aside, for a few blissful days. I generally start off summer vacation with very ambitious plans. I keep a list of things to accomplish. So far, I've kept my current list since about 1995. The only item I've been able to check off is "Make list of things to accomplish in summer." I get to the cottage and suddenly feel that life is giving me permission to do the things I dream of all year: relax and do nothing. The idea of "leisure activity" seems the ultimate oxymoron. In my mind, right up there with "too much coffee."

Even in August, though, it isn't possible to deny every little inconvenience of life. There's a reason for this: it's my birthday month. Every year I have to face the fact that, once again, I did not become prime minister or marry Harrison Ford.

It is my belief that those of us with summer birthdays are owed something by the world in general. I will hear no whining from people who are born on Christmas Day — you, after all, are in pretty illustrious company. And I have a friend born on New Year's Eve who always claims the parties are for her. Those of us with July or August birthdays alone know the grief of having our special day overshadowed by a two-month-long celebration of decent weather.

When I was growing up, I never had a birthday party because all of my friends were out of town in August. Then suddenly, the summer I turned 9, my parents threw me a huge bash. There was a clown and a magician and even a pony to ride. I have no idea where the guests came from; maybe they rented them too. In any case, it was a thrilling day and I took this as a sign of birthday parties to come. The next summer I was sent off to camp for the month of August and I didn't have a birthday at home again until I was 21.

I am not one of those people who passes 40 and says, "No more birthday parties!" There is a reason to share this occasion with family and friends: they give you stuff. I believe in the adage "It's better to give than receive." So really, marking my birthday is my way of allowing those I love to have the fun part.

Perhaps, in some ways, those of us with summer birthdays really have it better. It's hard to fret about what you haven't accomplished in your life when you're too relaxed to care about what you haven't accomplished that day.

My few weeks at the cottage each summer help me stay calm and stress-free when I return to the city — for about the first 15 minutes. After that, "relaxed" applies only to the style of my jeans. "Stress-free" is no longer an option. I remember one autumn afternoon a few years back, when I suddenly realized that the laundry was done and put away, the house was clean, dinner was in the fridge and the kids weren't due home from school for another half-hour. It was the most incredible feeling; I had no idea what to do with myself.

There's a reason why I don't generally relax more; it's hard work. I can't watch TV unless I'm folding laundry. I can't chat on the phone unless I'm making dinner. As my mother would say, "I can't relax unless I'm doing something."

When I was growing up, relaxing seemed more of a scheduled part of life. Sunday, in particular, was a day of rest; there was no option to go to a mall or a hardware store or a garden centre. Fortunately, enlightened social policy now makes it possible for us to be just as stressed on Sunday as we are every other day of the week. I have to admit, I sometimes wonder if this is really progress. My friend Avi observes the ancient Jewish ritual of Shabbat. From sundown on Friday to sundown on Saturday, Avi doesn't shop or answer the telephone or use his computer. The most astonishing part of this to me is that things in his life still get done.

Avi's observance of Shabbat makes me feel that I really don't understand how to use time. It reminds me of the summer I spent working in Prince Edward Island. I would make an appointment to meet someone in "city time" meaning: "2:15 p.m., unless I'm really late, in which case it might be 2:25." My Island friends would suggest, "You do what you have to do and I'll do what I have to do and then we'll kind of meet up." Somehow, it always worked.

There are a few things I do know about time. One is that it goes faster when I'm reading a book than when I'm listening to my daughter practise her trumpet. The hallmark of a successful rehearsal is when I can make out what piece she's attempting to play.

Another thing is that time only seems to stand still. When

my children, Matt and Becky, were preschoolers, my mother would say, "Enjoy these days, they're over so soon." And, most days, all I could think was, "Not soon enough." Time with toddlers is a summer afternoon; it lasts forever and ends far too quickly.

I know that trying to do two things at once makes time seem to go even faster, but doing one thing at a time has been out of the question for years. When my children were babies, I could accomplish any household task with one hand while I cradled the baby in the other. Life had never been more hectic. I called my mother one day and asked if she could come over to look after the kids for a while because "I've just been so stressed; I've spent my whole week rushing around." It was great when Mom arrived; finally, a few hours to get things done.

Frantic activity has a price. Matt was about three weeks old when I took him grocery shopping with me for the first time. I was amazing. I mastered a baby car-seat lock that would have stymied Houdini. I comparison shopped, making snap decisions. I got everything on my list, hauled it out to the car and paused for a moment to marvel at how really well I'd handled all of this — just long enough to realize I'd left the baby on the checkout counter.

As the kids got older, life didn't seem any less hectic. There is a philosophy of time that says that this day-to-day time continuum is simply an illusion. In fact, everything happens at the same time. This is certainly true in my house on any weekday morning. Time may fly when you're having fun but it positively takes the Concorde when you have to pick up groceries, get to work or the drugstore or the dentist or the dry cleaner, zip back across town to the computer supplies shop and be home to pick up the kids for lunch.

I have also learned that:

1. The speed of time is relative. When you're with relatives, it goes more slowly.

2. The amount of time spent assisting a child with a school project over the weekend is directly proportionate to the likelihood of their remembering on Sunday night that it's not due for another two weeks.

3. Baseball game time is different from hockey game time which is nothing at all like basketball game time. This is about all I do know about sports. I am perfectly capable of reading an entire article in the newspaper that refers to team names, player names and still not have a clue what sport they're talking about.

What I've begun to realize, though, is that I do have enough hours in the day; I just have too many things to do in them. Maybe I'm not a "slave to the clock," but sometimes I'm held captive by my own desire to have a spotless kitchen or an up-to-date e-mail correspondence or a full roster of social activities. Maybe, just maybe, if I put a few of those things aside in the new season ahead, I'll find I have time for everything . . . that matters.

It's impossible to deny that autumn is on the way now. I have to pull on a sweatshirt in the evening to watch the kids in their final swim of the summer. Tomorrow morning, we'll pack the car and head back to the city once more.

School is still weeks away, but this summer is already more about memories than plans. Even now, the kids are feeling that surge of excitement at the year beginning again — the rush of school and social life and activities. Some days, I know, the demands on my time will seem more than the hours and energy I have to give. Hard as I try to lead my own life, it will often seem to be rushing by me. And the more I try to pack into a day, the faster the minutes will seem to slip away.

Or, perhaps, they won't. In a few weeks, the trees in my tiny backyard will once again throw a comforter of red and gold leaves across my lawn. I can savour the colours even as I rake far too many bags. In November, the wind will be sharp against my cheek as Sparky and I brave cold mornings in the dog park. On deep December evenings, holiday lights will brush stained-glass patterns onto newly fallen snow. And in the spring, sun-warmed breezes will blow confetti petals from the cherry tree outside my work-room window — a celebration of nature awakening once more. I can see all these things. I can hold the memories in my heart. And, in those rare and treasured moments when I can sit quietly for a moment with a good book or a cup of tea, or a child's head in my lap, I will know that sometimes time does lie down and is still for us. And then we return to the world, to begin again.

Acting Our Age

Years ago, I made a vow with myself that I was going to age gracefully, embrace the changes in my body as they occurred and celebrate the natural process of life rather than clinging ridiculously to the blush of youth. Now that I'm over 40, that's exactly what I plan to do . . . in about 10 or 20 years. In the meantime, I'm clinging on for all I'm worth.

I was concerned to discover recently, however, that getting older is not only a state of mind, but it also appears to be the state of my thighs as well. I don't mind cellulite, exactly. After all, it's hereditary. Finally, something I can blame on my mother. But it seems that if I want to maintain the appearance of youth, it may be time to do something radical. I mean, other than exercising or changing my eating habits. That would be too radical.

A little research proved that there are a lot of choices about how to deal with the aging process. Just no good ones. In the case of my cellulite, for instance, I can either take the medical treatment route — including worrisome chemicals, creams or tablets — or the more sensible healthy approach— I just won't wear shorts ever again.

I decided against going to a "nip, tuck and suck" clinic. I'm sure it would be like the time we decided to buy new towels for the bathroom and ended up renovating the second floor. Sure, I could have my cellulite siphoned but, eventually, I'm bound to think of something else I'd like to have done — probably before I'm off the operating table. Besides, after looking into what is really involved, I found that I have a fundamental problem with this kind of treatment: I can't afford it — $6,000 for perkier breasts, $4,000 for smoother thighs. One surgeon I consulted assured me, "It will change your life." It's true. I would be very, very poor.

What my research also taught me is that a big part of fighting the age battle is to look after my health. If you feel better, you look better, the age-old wisdom goes. (No wonder I look fabulous after a glass or two of red wine.) So, I decided not to do anything foolish. Instead, I would go to an anti-aging clinic. There's one on every corner these days.

OK, yes, anti-aging clinic sounds a bit like a "Hold Back the Tides" clinic or "Make Yourself a Foot Taller" clinic. The philosophy of these places, though, is that rather than provide superficial temporary solutions to aging, they strive for "optimum health" for a longer life. In other words, they won't make me look any better, but they'll increase the number of years I'll have to look worse. Something like that.

I found the material I received in the mail very comforting. It turns out that many, many people are choosing to buy this kind of anti-aging, alternative health service. Mind you, many people buy things such as garden gnomes and Nortel stock too, but that didn't faze me for an instant.

It was easy to see from reading this material that private health care really is more evolved than our publicly funded institutions. This clinic offers not only health assessments and procedures, but also a full range of European skin-care treatments. I can get a collagen anti-wrinkle eye treatment at the same time as I'm giving a urine sample.

There were inspirational quotes such as "Medicine is for the people. It is not for the profits," followed by a notice that missed appointments would be billed at a rate of $150 each. You can't put a price on good health, but this place was certainly prepared to give it a try. A full assessment, not including the subsequent treatments, was $3,000. I was reminded of all the times I have approached the more expensive cosmetic counters chanting, "I'm worth it," only to see the prices and deciding "Well, possibly not." Three thousand dollars seemed like a lot of money to have someone tell me what's wrong with me. I have relatives who will do it for nothing.

I opted for the mini-assessment plan, which cost about $400. For that, I would still get a "biological terrain assessment" and they would check the state of my free radicals. It was very impressive. Before this, I would have thought free radicals was the name of a college political society. Instead, I find that they are "highly reactive molecules with an unsatisfied electron valence pair." Apparently, the deterioration of my free radicals was likely interfering with the intervention of my anti-oxidants at that very moment. I was torn between immediately calling for an appointment or using this as the plot for my first science fiction novel. I called and begged for the earliest possible assessment.

The last thing I did was check the credentials of the doctor in charge of the clinic. According to the information sent, he had virtually no clinical experience in traditional medicine but did have years of practice as a psychiatrist. This was helpful because by the end of the time I spent there, I realized that what I needed was to have my head examined.

The Questionnaire

Before going for my assessment, I was asked to fill out sheets detailing my current diet, exercise plan and lifestyle. I found the lifestyle questions somewhat lacking. For instance, "Do you have stress related to relationships?" could have read simply "Do you have relationships?"

There was a nutritional information sheet, which advised me to eat fruit and vegetables raw as often as possible. Apparently, cooking is not a good idea. I never thought is was. The clinic provided a "glycemic index" that rates certain foods on how they affect blood-sugar levels in the body. I could tell from this chart that eating a big bowl of corn syrup was probably not a good idea. Sponge cake rates 46 on the scale. Chickpeas score 33. There were no serving sizes indicated, so I went wild envisioning how much I could have. Perhaps the rating system could be interpreted as meaning that six chickpeas are 33 and an entire sponge cake is 46. So, half a sponge cake is only 23 — much better than eating six chickpeas. This diet advice was making me feel better already.

The Assessment

The minute I walk into the waiting room, I can tell this clinic is a classy place. My GP has a receptionist whose entire job description seems to be to ignore people standing in front of her for as long as possible. Here they have three receptionists doing that. Eventually, I am escorted into an examination room and handed a paper gown. I was a bit put out. For $400, I expected Anne Klein at least.

I'll never understand the wisdom of sticking someone in a small room with fluorescent lighting, making them take off their clothes, wrap themselves in a paper towel and then expect to get an accurate reading of their temperature and blood pressure. In this case, my blood pressure was taken by a computer. It clicked and beeped and whirled and spit out my reading. After all that, the technician got out the standard arm pump and tested me again "in case the computer is wrong," she explained.

The technician described the herbal detox program I'd be doing during the weeks that I wait for my test results and said I could buy the supplies I needed from the three officious receptionists.

"But you don't know if there's anything wrong with me, yet."

She sighed sagely, "There's always something."

Next, I stood on a metal scale that the technician programmed with my height. Two numbers appeared on the screen: my weight and 33. "That's your percentage of body fat," she explained. I was amazed. Particularly since, given only my height and weight, this machine could as easily review my stock portfolio as figure out my body-fat ratio. I asked how it manages this. The technician didn't know but she did suggest, "It should be 22. You have to lose some weight." Now, I am of a body type classically referred to as "a little on the scrawny side." The only way I could drop 10 pounds would be to donate some vital organs.

Later, I asked another technician about the scale. "Oh no. It measures muscle content. You must have too much muscle." I knew it. My rigorous daily exercise routine of getting up and down from the computer several times to get coffee had finally caught up with me. I made a mental note to improve my health by buying a cappuccino maker for my workroom. Finally, the clinic head assured me that the scale did indeed measure percentage of fat and worked by shooting painless electronic charges through my body. There is a saying that "the truth shall set you free." But sometimes, in fact, the truth just makes you queasy.

Next came the hair sample test. The clinic material says that taking body hair to test for a variety of conditions is widely used in forensic medicine. This makes perfect sense to me because, frankly, this test almost killed me.

To obtain an accurate hair analysis, a sizable hair sample is required. One of the surly receptionists was dispatched to seat me on a stool and then hack chunks of hair from the back of my head — enough to tip a small scale. I lost it. I mean, I'm sorry, but you could wax my entire body in February and not get enough hair to tip that scale. On top of that, I had just treated myself to a really decent cut, colour and condition and this woman was lopping off about $5 worth of hair with every snip. I didn't care if I was failing "patient." I got out of the chair, announcing loudly that I was prepared to sacrifice good health for being able to wear my hair in a ponytail sometime in the next five years. The receptionist grumbled. "We have to test you. How are we supposed to tell if you're anxious or stressed?" Let me save you time. I wasn't before I started this procedure.

The waiting period to see the doctor and review my test results was three weeks — perhaps to give me a chance to calm down. We sat together in a tiny office. This was a real doctor in my books. Mature, with tousled salt-and-pepper hair and just a little rumpled around the edges. Soft lines around his eyes from nights of sitting at the bedside of feverish elderly patients or helping women through child-birth. Then I remembered he's a psychiatrist. OK, well, he still looks impressive. The doctor mused over stacks of my test results for a moment, sighing deeply. He flipped through some graphs and shook his head in kindly concern. I got the good news first. My vital organs are functioning. What a relief. Most of my tests showed that I'm within the normal range by common medical standards.

The doctor wiped his eyes and informed me sadly that medical standards are not high enough. *Canada's Food Guide to Healthy Eating* is useful for warding off scurvy at best. Vegetables now contain 60 percent less nutrition than they did 20 years ago and, on top of that, my test results included phrases such as "The rH2 value of the blood indicates that a relative concentration of electron donors to electron acceptors has decreased." All of this combined is very bad. Or possibly bad. As I age, I may experience a decrease in the functioning of my kidneys or thyroid gland. I'd say that's a pretty good bet.

There was more good news. The doctor launched into a plan for chelation therapy, the specialty of this particular clinic, guaranteed to buck me right up — in 10 to 20 sessions at $150 each, along with creams and an extensive list of homeopathic supplements. I am a great believer in homeopathic remedies. Generally, though, I like to have them prescribed by a homeopath.

The bottom line on this is that I had paid $400 to find out that, with the exception of urgently needing an unproven medical treatment for a condition no government-sanctioned GP would recognize, I am an average healthy woman. Oh, and my biological age is between 40 and 50. I am 44. So, do I feel foolish? Well . . . yes and no. Frankly, if $400 is all I spend in my lifetime trying to ward off the effects of the aging process, it'll show I'm a much wiser person than I suspected.

In the end, I think if this doctor had wanted to help me age well, he could have said something like this: "You know what? You're going to age. Eat properly. Have a piece of cheesecake now and then. Get your exercise from doing something you enjoy. Get a little sun on your face, but not too much. The things of age will be different than the things of youth. Youth may have beauty and energy because it doesn't have much else. Savour each stage of life instead of clinging to the ones you've outgrown. Live as long as possible. But also, live now." Help like that will never pay for advertising, clinics or receptionists. But really, it's advice I can live with.

The Right Stuff

Every now and then I like to take time to reflect on past mistakes. And not only those of other people. If it's true that we learn from our mistakes, I ought to have a Ph.D. by now.

Years ago, when I was in high school the television program *Saturday Night Live* occasionally featured cartoons that starred a Plasticine character named Mr. Bill. Terrible things happened to Mr. Bill. He got blown up and stomped on; his life was one long session of undeserved pain and suffering. As a teenager, I related to this.

To celebrate our friend Bill Stone's 17th birthday, my best friend, Mary, and I decided to bake a Mr. Bill cake. Three layers of gluey fudge cake, oceans of chocolate frosting and, on top, a picture of Mr. Bill in glorious three-tone tube icing. As a finishing touch, we tucked a small red firecracker into the figure. The idea, which anyone who has ever combined baking with pyrotechnics will see immediately, was that when we lit the firecracker, the figure would neatly "pop" and it would be very festive. That evening, our friends gathered around the table in Mary's parents' kitchen. The match was struck, the firecracker wick flamed and 10 pounds of chocolate cake exploded in every direction.

Looking back, I wonder who could really call this incident a mistake. OK, possibly Mary's mother who was still finding icing in the light fixtures 10 years later. But I prefer to focus on the valuable life lessons I learned from this experience — such as food that explodes is probably not a good idea, and neither is letting teenagers do anything.

I hope that by remembering the mistakes of my past I will not repeat them. Except, of course, for the enjoyable ones. I do take time to reflect on important life questions such as, "Where did I fall short, get off track, waste time?" Did I, for example, apply myself this past week and get my work done or did I sit around watching *Columbo* reruns? I have to continually remind myself of what I want out of life. Otherwise sometimes I miss my *Columbo* reruns.

Taking time to consider past events means that I don't make the same mistakes twice. Instead, I make all new ones. I now have a life list of "things that struck me as a good idea at the time even though all my friends saw disaster coming a mile off." The list includes such things as: planning a perfect wedding and then thinking it might be fun to invite my relatives, and any scheme that involved buying a plant. Then there are the less obvious but equally doomed ideas, like taking a family driving vacation.

Two summers ago, my ex-husband, Michael, and I decided to take our children, Matt and Becky, on a road trip through Quebec. I have to admit, at the time I wondered if travelling together was a surefire recipe for two weeks of hostility and bickering. Between the kids, I mean. My ex and I get along fine.

This was not our first family driving vacation, which just proved one thing: we should have known better. Years ago, we drove to South Carolina. I packed snacks, books, art projects and armed myself with lists of fun places to stop along the way. The only thing the kids remember about the trip is Mom being pulled over for speeding outside Myrtle Beach.

For our Quebec trip, we thought we'd try something new. We rented a recreational vehicle. Neither Michael nor I had ever driven an RV before. We had never been in an RV. I think the best either of us could have done was to pick out an RV in a police lineup.

We did learn from this trip. We learned that the French phrase for "trunk open" is not *frein à main*, which means "parking brake." We discovered that if you do not hot-glue things to the counter of an RV, they will fly off and hit you in the back of the head when you pull out of the campsite. Every time. We also found out that Michael and I are mature enough to weather difficult, unfamiliar experiences and still be speaking to each other — eventually.

I think the life lesson in all of this is that there is a way to avoid making mistakes: never do anything new. But the times I've ended up with egg, or cake, on my face are the times I've ended up a little wiser and with the satisfaction at least of having dared. So when it comes to new experiences, perhaps the only mistake I can really make is not to try.